PSYCHOEDUCATIONAL GROUPS

PSYCHOEDUCATIONAL GROUPS

Nina W. Brown, Ed.D.

ACCELERATED DEVELOPMENT

A member of the Taylor & Francis Group

USA	Publishing Office:	ACCELERATED DEVELOPMENT *A member of the Taylor & Francis Group* 325 Chestnut Street Philadelphia, PA 19106 Tel: (215) 625-8900 Fax: (215) 625-2940
	Distribution Center:	ACCELERATED DEVELOPMENT *A member of the Taylor & Francis Group* 1900 Frost Road, Suite 101 Bristol, PA 19007-1598 Tel: (215) 785-5800 Fax: (215) 785-5515
UK		Taylor & Francis Ltd. 1 Gunpowder Square London EC4A 3DE Tel: 171 583 0490 Fax; 171 583 0581

PSYCHOEDUCATIONAL GROUPS

1 2 3 4 5 6 7 8 9 0   G H B   98

This book was set in Times Roman by Sherri W. Emmons. Edited by Sherri W. Emmons. Technical development by Cindy Long.

A CIP catalog record for this book is available from the British Library.
  ∞ The paper in this publication meets the requirements of the ANSI Standard Z39.48-1984 (Permanence of Paper)

Library of Congress Cataloging-in-Publication Data

Brown, Nina W.
    Psychoeducational groups / Nina W. Brown.
        p.   cm.
    Includes bibliographical references and index.
    ISBN 1-56032-676-X (paper : alk. paper)
    1. Mental health counseling. 2. Group counseling. 3. Small groups. 4. Life skills--Study and training. I. Title.
    RC466.B76   1998
    362.2'04256--dc21   97–43840
                                                          CIP

ISBN: 1-56032-676-X (paper)

DEDICATION

This book is dedicated to Samantha and Christopher, the new additions to the family.

CONTENTS

CHAPTER 11
WORK-RELATED PSYCHOEDUCATIONAL GROUPS   199

CHAPTER 12
SELF-HELP AND SUPPORT GROUPS   237

INTRODUCTION

The reasons for writing this book are many, but the most important one is the need for a resource for students in group classes. While the book focuses on psychoeducational groups for human service workers, other mental health professionals—such as counselors in schools, organizational trainers, alcohol and drug education and treatment professionals, and support group organizers—will find it useful as well.

This book was developed as a resource for planning, conducting, and evaluating psychoeducational groups. There are many resources available that address topics for psychoeducational groups (e.g., anger management), present theories of learning and principles of instruction, and aim to develop group leadership skills. I have found no resources, however, that combine all three of these components. This book seeks to fill that gap.

Further, students reported that many of their jobs required them to conduct psychoeducational groups, and the requirements for human service workers and other mental health professionals pointed out a need for preparation in leading psychoeducational groups as contrasted with counseling and therapy groups. The trend toward briefer group counseling highlights the need for psychoeducational groups.

FORMAT OF THIS BOOK

This book is designed to prepare leaders for a variety of psychoeducational groups. I start with the assumption that there are basic skills and strategies that are consistent for all groups, all participant populations, and all group issues. These basics are presented in chapters 2 through 8.

Chapters 9 through 11 focus on developing psychoeducational groups around specific topics and for a variety of populations. Examples of games, exercises, mini-lectures, and handouts are presented around a topic for education groups, social skills groups and work-related groups. Chapter 12 deals with self-help/support groups. Following is an overview for each chapter.

Chapter 1 describes psychoeducational groups by size, management of content, length of group, responsibility of leader, severity of problems, competence of leader, prevention versus remediation, and personal issues involvement. Psychoeducational groups can be distinguished in four other ways: structured verses unstructured, personal versus abstract, developmental versus remedial, and open versus closed membership. Examples of placement for different psychoeducational groups along a continuum are provided. Differences between psychoeducational groups and counseling/therapy groups also are presented.

Chapter 2 provides an overview of learning theories and principles of instruction. Psychoeducational groups emphasize learning more than personal growth or insight. Their primary focus is the presentation of new material, ways of relating, or new behaviors.

The chapter summarizes major learning theories, such as conditioning, mediation-stimulus-response, social learning, and insight. The principles of learning also are presented.

Guidelines for instruction focus on presenting material in group. Principles such as readiness, motivation, active involvement, organization, Bloom's taxonomy, the efficacy of techniques, and media are discussed.

Chapter 3 describes the characteristics and skills of effective leaders. Characteristics are such thing as belief in group process, willingness to admit mistakes, flexibility, tolerance of ambiguity, self-awareness, caring, warmth, and genuineness. Examples of skills are reflection, clarifying, summarizing, blocking, and terminating. Examples of ineffective communicating also are described.

Chapter 4 focuses on problem participants, the goals for their behavior, and involuntary group members. Problem behaviors and their goals are categorized in three groups: overparticipation (e.g., monopolizing), underparticipation (e.g., withdrawing or silent), and socializing (e.g., distracting behavior).

Involuntary group members range from students in training groups as part of their degree studies to incarcerated felons or psychiatric inpatients. Constraints to active participation, group leader strategies, and ethical considerations are discussed.

The chapter also discusses how to relate leader strategies to participants' levels. Levels refer to knowledge, readiness, and maturity, not education or intellect. For example, when participants are at a low level of knowledge about the subject, the leader must use more directing and structuring strategies. Even very bright and well-educated participants will begin at the low level.

Chapter 5 focuses on major ethical issues and helpful group factors. Sixteen ethical issues (such as dual relationships, coercion and pressure, leaving a group) are discussed with recommendations for the group leader. The helpful group factors are divided into most likely to appear (e.g., universality, altruism, and imparting of information), likely to appear (e.g., interpersonal learning, development of socializing techniques, instillation of hope, and cohesiveness), and unlikely to appear (e.g., catharsis, recapitualization of the family of origin, and existential factors) in the psychoeducational group.

Chapter 6 introduces conflict management strategies based on the maturity, expertise, and level of responsibility assumed by group members. Conflicts between members, between a member and the leader, and between the group and the leader are all expected to arise, and strategies to cope effectively are presented. Guidelines for construction confrontation are described.

Chapter 7 describes group stages and how the leader can recognize and capitalize on them. Groups always have a beginning and an end—two distinct stages. The conflict and working stages usually are present, even when unrecognized. The group leader is presented with specific strategies for identification and use of group stages.

Chapter 7 also addresses preplanning, understanding the needs of participants, the role of experiential activities, and tasks for the leader. Suggestions are given for increasing participants' activity and interactions when the group is large and for increasing personalized learning and satisfaction.

Chapter 8 is devoted to differentiating between games and exercises, appropriate uses for each, the relationship of learning theory to both, and examples of both games and exercises. Attention is given to planning, conducting, and processing these experiences. Descriptions of simulations and role play also are provided.

Exercises and games make use of learning theories by providing opportunities for repetition, reinforcement, associations, use of the senses, and personal meaningfulness. Material presented in this way is more likely to be retained and applied.

This chapter includes examples of exercises and games that can be used with small or large groups and with members of all ages. These usually are not dependent on the educational level of participants. The examples are classified as icebreakers, team building, attending to task, nonverbal communication, having fun, and termination.

Specific guidelines are given for planning, selecting materials, leader preparation, introducing content, and helping participants to get the most out of their experiences.

Chapter 9 presents basic guidelines for groups with educational objectives and goals. Specific considerations when developing groups for children and adolescents are discussed with an example exercise given for each.

Two complete programs are presented, complete with exercises, handouts, and mini-lectures. The first program, "Study Skills," is designed for adolescents, although much of the content could be adapted easily for children and adults. The second program, "Communications," is designed for adults to become more aware of effective and ineffective communications. Exercises and mini-lectures could be modified for adolescents.

Chapter 10 begins with a description of some outcomes for social and life skills training groups with a variety of populations ranging from children to adults and from psychiatric patients to managers. The program presented in this chapter focuses on developing social skills and can be used with children, adolescents, and adults. Modifications would make the exercises appropriate for a variety of populations.

Chapter 11 presents an example for a work-related psychoeducational group. Since these groups are usually designed for working adults, the introduction focuses on preparation for this particular target audience. The "Time Management" program can be tailored for the target audience, as the exercises, handouts, and mini-lectures deal with issues directly related to that particular work site.

Chapter 12 provides information to help a leader distinguish between most self-help and support groups, with suggestions for conducting sessions. These groups tend to be more counseling in nature, but have a significant psychoeducational component.

ACKNOWLEDGMENTS

I want to express my appreciation to Jean Lederle, whose word-processing skills make my job much easier, and to my students, who gave me feedback on chapter drafts. Appreciation also goes to Jim Cross, Dean of Engineering at Old Dominion University, and William Drewry, Chair of the Civil and Environmental Engineering Department at Old Dominion University, for their continued support and encouragement. None of this would be possible without the assistance of my family, who provide inspiration, with special thanks to my husband, Wilford.

Chapter 1

PSYCHOEDUCATIONAL GROUPS—AN OVERVIEW

There are a variety of groups conducted every day for many different audiences. Many are counseling or therapy groups, but most fall into the psychoeducational group category. Psychoeducational groups usually are considered similar to guidance groups (Gladding, 1995); guidance groups, in turn, typically are thought of as being for children in school settings.

However, I use the term *psychoeducational group* in this book to include a broad spectrum of groups that have a significant educational component; such groups are used with children, adolescents, and adults in all kinds of settings, including hospitals, businesses, universities, governmental and social service agencies, and the military.

The definition of psychoeducational groups adopted by the Association for Specialists in Group Work (ASGW, 1991) addresses the importance of educational and prevention goals in such groups. These groups serve to educate those facing a potential threat or a developmental life event (i.e, retirement), or to teach coping skills to those dealing with an immediate life crisis. The ASGW defined the goal for such groups as "preventing an array of educational and psychological disturbance from occurring" (Gladding, 1995, p. 436).

This book focuses on the theory and practice of psychoeducational groups and starts with the assumption that these groups are provided for all ages and educational levels in practically every setting. Another basic assumption is that the groups emphasize education or learning, rather than self-awareness and self-understanding. The cognitive component takes precedence over the affec-

1

tive component; indeed, for some groups the affective component may be completely absent.

PSYCHOEDUCATIONAL GROUPS IN THERAPY

Psychoeducational groups are primarily educational and emphasize skills training. However, they also can contribute significantly to group counseling/therapy and to group psychotherapy, as demonstrated by the following studies:

In a meta-analysis of 191 studies, Devine (1992) confirmed the efficacy of psychoeducational care for adult surgical patients.

Thomas la Salivia (1993) proposed enhancing addiction treatment through psychoeducational groups.

Gamble, Elder, and Lashley (1989, p. 71) reviewed studies on the use of psychoeducational groups in the treatment of eating disorders, depression, and alcohol abuse. Although the studies lacked adequate control groups, the treatments were found to be effective.

Forester, Cornfield, Fleiss, and Thomas (1993) used a psychoeducational component in their group work with cancer patients, as did Fawzy and Fawzy (1994) and Fawzy, Fawzy, Aront, and Pasnau (1995).

Psychoeducational groups also can be used in pregroup preparation sessions, in which prospective group members are taught what to expect in therapy and how to be effective group members. Yalom (1995) reviewed research on the efficacy of pregroup preparation and found that prepared members exhibited less anxiety, participated more, had lower drop-out rates, showed an improved ability to communicate, expressed more emotions, and had better attendance rates.

These are but a few examples showing the usefulness of psychoeducational groups in therapy. While such groups are not considered to *be* therapy, they do have therapeutic usefulness.

CONCEPTUALIZATION OF PSYCHOEDUCATIONAL GROUPS

For our purposes here, psychoeducational groups are defined as those that have educational, skill-development, and/or task-accomplishment goals. Some groups may have overlapping goals; that is, they may incorporate more than one goal.

The ASGW, a division of the American Counseling Association, has developed separate lists of skills and knowledge for leaders of task and work groups, psychoeducational groups, counseling groups, and psychotherapy groups. In addition, the ASGW (1991) has developed guidelines for core group work training considered basic to specialty areas. The association's definitions for psychoeducational groups and for task and work groups have been combined in this book under the umbrella of psychoeducational groups. In addition, self-help groups are included as well, as many of these have strong, significant educational components.

Before discussing the knowledge and competencies needed to conduct psychoeducational groups, let me distinguish between psychoeducational groups and counseling/therapy groups. Table 1.1 presents an overview of major differences between the two.

DEFINITIONS

Psychoeducational groups range from discussion groups to self-help groups. Sessions may be held in organizations, businesses, churches, schools, detention homes, jails, colleges and universities, community centers, governmental agencies, or even private homes. These groups also cover all ages, from children through the elderly, and they may be preventive or remedial in focus. Leaders of psychoeducational groups should have basic preparation to lead a variety of groups for different age levels in practically any setting. A process for extending knowledge and learning new skills is discussed in chapter 3.

Educational/Task Groups

Educational/task groups are formed around a common purpose, usually a task to be achieved. The emphasis is on increasing members' knowledge about a particular topic or subject, and the group includes considerable discussion of opinions and ideas. Examples of groups in this category are discussion groups, study groups, task forces, volunteer groups, civic organizations, and committees. Most of these groups have designated or elected leaders. Leaders who have an understanding of group dynamics and leadership skills can help educational/task groups conduct their business more effectively and efficiently.

TABLE 1.1
Comparison of Psychoeducational and Counseling/Therapy Groups

Psychoeducational Groups	Counseling/Therapy Groups
Emphasize didactic and instruction	Emphasize experiential and feelings
Use planned, structured activities	Little use of these
Goals usually defined by leader	Group members define goals
Leader operates as facilitator, teacher	Leader guides, intervenes, protects
Focus on prevention	Focus on self-awareness, remediation
No screening of members	Screening and orientation to group expected prior to beginning group
Cannot set limits on number in group	Can set limits on number in group
Group can be very large (e.g., 50)	Usually limited to 5 to 10 members
Self-disclosure accepted but not encouraged—nor is it the focus	Self-disclosure is expected
Privacy and confidentiality not primary concerns or emphasis	Privacy and confidentiality critical, basic elements
Sessions may be limited to one	Usually consists of several sessions
Task functions emphasized	Maintenance functions emphasized over task

Educational/Guidance Groups

Educational/guidance groups focus on providing information to help participants cope with a crisis, developmental issues, or prevention of problems. Dissemination of information is important for these groups, and the information usually is focused on a particular topic, such as job search skills. Examples of groups in this category are career education groups and groups focused on alcohol education or learning about an illness, such as cancer, choosing a college major, or developing study skills. Leaders must have teaching skills in addition to understanding group dynamics and group leadership skills.

Training/Work Groups

Training/work groups are those initiated to meet work expectations or demands. They usually provide information on work processes, structuring for team development, or how a job or task can be performed more efficiently. Often these groups are formed around a perceived need identified by the employer. Such groups might focus on time-management, team-building, specific skills (such as computer networking), or other task-related activities. Leaders have a significant teaching role for all of these groups and a strong facilitative role for some (such as team building).

Training/Relations Groups

Training/relations groups may stand alone or bridge training/work groups or training/social skills groups, as these groups can have subject matter germane to all three (e.g., communication skills). Both communication and interpersonal relations play parts in task and relations groups. The leader teaches new ways of communicating and relating. These groups may focus on parenting, communication skills, interpersonal relations, work relationships, getting along with supervisors, changing personal relationships, divorce, and so on. While there is a significant information dissemination component, there also is a significant personal issues component. The leader needs to have knowledge and expertise to balance both.

Training/Social Skills Groups

Training/social skills groups focus on developing social skills and can be either preventive or remedial. Most are formed in response to observed detrimental behaviors, such as violence. These groups tend to have both education and personal issues components and rely in part on experiential activities, such as practicing new behaviors. These groups may focus on conflict mediation, anger management, social skills development, and so on. Leaders need expertise in setting up and conducting experiences (e.g., role-play) and in presenting information and facilitating the group process.

CLASSIFICATION

Table 1.2 classifies groups by their primary purpose: education, skills training, or self-understanding/self-knowledge. There will be considerable overlap of purposes for some groups (e.g., communication skills), but it is helpful for the leader to remember the primary purpose for the group so that the focus can be maintained.

TABLE 1.2
Classification and Differentiation of Psychoeducational Groups

Differentiation Categories	Education/ Task	Education/ Guidance	Training			Support
			Work	Relations	Social	
Purpose						
education	high	high	moderate	moderate	moderate	moderate to low
skills training	low	low to moderate	high	high	high	low
self-knowledge	low	low to moderate	low	moderate to high	high	high to moderate
Size	moderate to large	moderate to large	moderate to large	low to moderate	low	large
Mgt. of Content						
leader directed	xxx	xx	x	x	xx	x
outside forces	x	x	xx	x	x	x
charged mgt.	x	x	x	xxx	xx	xxx
Length of Group						
one session	xx	xxx	xxx	x	x	x
2 to 8 sessions	xxx	xx	xx	xxx	xxx	xx
8+ sessions	x	x	x	xx	xx	xxx
Leader Responsibility	high	high	high	moderate	moderate	low
Severity of Problem	none	slight	none	slight to moderate	moderate to high	moderate to high
Competency of Leader						
Psychoed. groups	slight	slight	slight	slight to moderate	moderate to high	moderate to high
Prevention						
Remediation	Prevention	Prevention	Prevention to Remediation	Remediation to Prevention	Remediation to Prevention	Remediation
Personal Issue						
Involvement	slight	slight to moderate	slight	moderate	moderate to high	high

Education, as a primary purpose, refers to learning new material via the *cognitive* mode, through lecture, discussion, and observation/participation. Dissemination of new material is the focus, with the leader doing much of the presenting. New ideas, concepts, and facts form much of the content for education-focused groups.

Skills-training groups have a strong *experiential* component: Participants are expected to practice the emphasized skills. The group leader is expected to model the desired skills and to structure experiences to help participants practice them. Feedback on progress is another important component of these groups.

Groups focused primarily on self-understanding/self-knowledge begin to overlap with counseling/therapy groups. However, these purposes are considered somewhat differently for psychoeducational groups. The understandings and knowledge gained are on a more superficial level, self-disclosure is not a requisite, resistances are not identified or worked through, and past relationships are not explored. The understandings and knowledge gained are expected to reassure the members, to give feedback on the impact on others of their behavior, or to build self-confidence.

BASIC CHARACTERISTICS

Size

Psychoeducational groups range in size from 5 to 50 or even 100 members. Some workshops and seminars that fall into the category of psychoeducational groups can have 50 or more participants. These larger groups are included because most of the characteristics of psychoeducational groups apply (for example, goals, content, and expected outcomes). Counseling/therapy groups usually are limited to 5 to 10 members, even when there is a co-leader. Groups with fewer than 5 members will find it difficult to develop a sense of cohesion. It is likely that a psychoeducational group leader will have large numbers of participants, rather than few.

Management of Content

All groups have some content. How that content is managed refers to the mode of presentation, the initiator, and processing.

Modes of presentation can include lectures, role-play, and demonstrations.

Leaders of all kinds of groups have responsibility for preplanning. In psychoeducational groups, the leader may solicit input from others into setting goals and structuring activities. **Initiators** may be the leader, individual members, supervisors, or the group as a whole.

Processing is the depth and extent to which emerged material is talked about in the group.

Length of Group

The length and duration of psychoeducational groups can vary widely, from one session lasting one to two hours to long-term, ongoing groups (such as self-help or support groups). Generally, education-focused groups have fewer sessions than skills-training or self-help groups. However, psychoeducational groups are characterized by the brevity of their sessions: Most employ short sessions over a brief time period.

Responsibilities of the Leader

Leaders of psychoeducational groups have the primary responsibility for forming the group and selecting activities and for the functioning of the group. There is some variation among the different types of groups for leader responsibilities, however, and group leaders may engage outside experts to help set group goals and select activities: For example, supervisors may help with team-building groups, probation officers with anger management groups, and counselors with career education groups. These experts may make suggestions or identify needs for participants.

Members seldom participate in goal setting for psychoeducational groups as leaders rarely have the luxury of a pregroup interview session.

Severity of Problem

Not all psychoeducational groups are problem-focused the way counseling and therapy groups are. Although some counseling groups are seen as prevention groups, the idea that there is a potential problem to prevent helps give these groups a problem focus. While some psychoeducational groups do have a problem focus, such as anger management, many others do not. For purposes of classification here, problems also will encompass topics and concerns. *Severity* includes impact on relationships and functioning, with *considerable impact* referring to an unaddressed problem or concern. Groups that have prevention as a focus will have a moderate to slight classification, because some members in these groups may have already experienced a negative impact on relationships and functioning.

Competence of the Leader

The competency of the group leader is determined by many factors: knowledge of group dynamics; basic counseling, communication, and group leadership skills; knowledge of human growth and development issues; specialized knowledge and skills (for example, in substance abuse, career development, or characterological disorders); training; and supervision. Leaders of psychoeducational groups need the same knowledge base and many of the same skills as do leaders of counseling and therapy groups. However, they use these skills in somewhat different ways.

Leaders of psychoeducational groups use their knowledge and skills to understand participants and their needs, while leaders of counseling/therapy groups build on their understanding for interventions, facilitation, and resolution of personal concerns, problems, and issues. Further, leaders of counseling/therapy groups need more extensive preparation than do leaders of psychoeducational groups.

Groups are classified below by their level of need for intervention, facilitation, or resolution of personal problems and issues.

Prevention Versus Remediation. *Prevention* assumes that there has not been a manifestation of behavior that is cause for concern, but there is a need for expanded knowledge, The justification for prevention is this: Developmental issues are likely to arise; these issues can be dealt with more easily if the individual knows what to expect and what processes to use. Prevention-focused groups are useful in such areas as learning to use time wisely, selecting a career, and learning parenting skills.

Remediation assumes there is a deficit. Deficits usually result in negative and less positive outcomes, because of behaviors, attitudes, or skills. Once the deficit has been identified, specific remedial procedures are implemented. Examples of remedial groups are self-help groups, anger management groups, and groups focused on building self-esteem.

Personal Issues Involvement (PII).   Personal issues involvement for psychoeducational groups ranges from low or slight to high or intense. Groups are classified by the extent of need for personal issues involvement to be a member of the group (see Figure 1.1). For example, little personal issues involvement is needed to be a member of a discussion or time management group. More involvement of personal issues is needed to be a member of a self-help or anger management group.

Personal		Abstract
Support groups	Guidance groups	Discussion groups
Social skills training	Conflict mediation	Seminars
Communication	Training groups	Staff-development
Relationship training	Committees	In-service

Figure 1.1. Classification by extent of personal issues involvement.

Another aspect of PII is self-disclosure. The level and extent of self-disclosure expected rise with the level and intensity of personal issues involvement. Participants are encouraged to engage in appropriate self-disclosure in all groups. However, self-disclosure is more intense in counseling/therapy groups than in psychoeducational groups.

When there is expected self-disclosure along with PII, the leader needs more expertise in order to use the information effectively, link it to the group process, and protect and support the group member.

CATEGORIES OF PSYCHOEDUCATIONAL GROUPS

Psychoeducational groups can be categorized in several different ways: structural versus unstructured, personal versus abstract, developmental versus remedial, and open versus closed. All of these polarities can be combined to form even more categories. Categories fall along a continuum and some types of groups can bridge categories. A brief description of categories follows.

Structured Versus Unstructured

All groups require planning if they are to run smoothly and accomplish members' objectives, but some are more structured than others. *Structured groups* are those in which the leader selects the activities, each activity has a particular goal, and the activities are primarily paper and pencil tasks designed to facilitate discussion about the topic. Group members have little or no involvement in selecting objectives and tasks.

Unstructured groups are at the other extreme. The leader (if there is one) does minimal structuring—just enough to ensure that the group gets off the ground and that members' objectives are addressed. Group members make most decisions about what they will do. Few, if any, paper and pencil activities are used. Self-help groups are good examples of unstructured groups. Figure 1.2 lists psychoeducational groups by their degree of structure.

Structured	Elements of Both	Unstructured
←		→
Training groups	Guidance groups	Support groups
Staff development	Discussion groups	
Team development	Social skills training	
Seminars	Conflict mediation	
	Communication/ Relationship training groups	
	Committees	
	In-service	

Figure 1.2. Classification on a continuum of structure.

Personal Versus Abstract

Personal groups deal with issues of self-awareness and also with the individual's issues or concerns. Self-disclosure is expected and encouraged in such groups. While a personal focus may be more closely associated with counseling/therapy groups, psychoeducational groups such as support groups and social skills training groups also have significant levels of personal involvement.

Abstract groups deal with topics that may hold personal interest for participants, but they do not ask for the same level of self-disclosure or self-involvement. Abstractness suggests an emotional distancing. The topics can be "talked about" with only mild emotional involvement or with none. Discussion groups, training groups (e.g., team building), and other educational groups cluster toward the abstract.

Developmental Versus Remedial

Developmental groups build on members' strengths, while *remedial groups* focus on overcoming weaknesses or deficits. Developmental groups are more preventive in nature. Capitalizing on existing strengths is much easier than remediating deficiencies.

A unique problem for the leader of a remediation group is that many of the participants are there involuntarily—that is, they do not choose to be there. Some members in fact deny even having deficiencies and resent having to attend the group. Examples of remediation groups are social skills training and conflict mediation groups. These same types of groups can be developmental if the participants are voluntary attendees and have not evidenced deficiencies in the areas, for example, by fighting.

Open Versus Closed

Open groups usually meet over an extended length of time with changing membership—that is, some members leave and new ones are admitted. *Closed groups* also can meet over extended times, but as members leave no new ones are admitted. Groups that are short-term usually are closed. Although there may be no prohibition against admission of new members, it is rare that new ones attend.

Support groups, skills-training groups, and discussion groups are examples of open groups. With open membership, the group is constantly renewing itself or, in some instances, remaining in or reverting back to the initial stage with the introduction of new members. A prime challenge facing the leader of an open group is making new members feel welcome, as the new member is faced with the task of fitting in to an already existing group. Figure 1.3 presents categorization by open or closed membership.

Open		**Closed**
←		→
Support Groups	Social Skills Training	Seminars
Committees	Communication	Training Group
Discussion	Relationship Training	Guidance Groups
	Conflict Mediation	
	Team-Building	
	Staff Development	

Figure 1.3. Classification by degree of open membership.

Chapter 2

LEARNING THEORY FOR PSYCHOEDUCATIONAL GROUPS

The principal thrust of psychoeducational groups is learning. Learning new information, developing new or increased skills, finding other ways of communicating or relating, increasing self-management skills, and personal development are some of the desired outcomes for participants. Since learning is so important in these groups, leaders should understand some of the common theories of human learning. These can help in planning activities, selecting information, developing attainable goals and objectives, and tailoring groups for participants.

What follows is an overview of the major theories of human learning, retention of learned material, and transfer of learning. Readers are encouraged to read more about these and other theories in order to gain a better understanding of how humans learn so as to increase the effectiveness of the psychoeducational groups they lead.

Table 2.1 presents a summary of some of the major theories on human learning. It also lists one or two key persons associated with each theory and some of the elements that have implications for teaching in psychoeducational groups.

TABLE 2.1
Overview of Major Learning Theories

Theory	Focus	Theories	Elements	Persons
Conditioning: S-R	Overt behavior stimulus - response	Connectionism Behaviorism	Conditioned reflexes or responses Reinforcement Operant conditioning	B. F. Skinner E. L. Thorndike J. B. Watson
S-O-R: Mediation Stimulus-Response	Internal processes (O) affect S-R	Trial and error Reinforcement Reciprocal inhibition	Need reduction Drive stimulus Reflection Weakening of old responses by new ones	C. Hull J. Dollard & N. E. Miller J. Wolpe
Social Learning	Purposive interaction of behavior, environment, and cognitions	Cognitive Field Social Learning	Verbal persuasion performance accomplishments Vicarious learning	K. Lewin E. C. Talman A. Bandura J. B. Rotter
Insight	Reorganization of old terms Recognition of patterns, interrelatedness of concepts Problem solving	Gestalt	Whole vs. parts Form, organization, configuration phenomenology	M. Wertheimer K. Koffka W. Kohler

THEORIES OF LEARNING

Conditioning as Learning

Conditional learning has its roots in work done by Pavlov (1849-1936), which resulted in the basic principles of "classical conditioning" theory. One principle postulates that the nearly simultaneous pairing of a given stimulus (S) to a response (R) results in learning because of *contiguity:* Things are learned because they occur together. However, the learned response must occur from repeated pairings of the stimulus and response.

Pavlov demonstrated conditioning when he taught dogs to salivate at the sound of a bell. He had paired the sound of the bell with food, so the dogs anticipated being fed when they heard the bell and salivated.

Conditioning must occur over time, and it is unlikely that it can be systematically carried out during the brief span of a psychoeducational group. A contribution can be made, however, by pairing learning with reward and pleasure. Over time and with continued pairings, learning will be associated with positive outcomes.

Learning as Problem Solving

Thorndike (1913) conceptualized learning as problem solving. He conducted animal experiments, primarily with cats, to develop his laws of forming stimulus-response (S-R) bonds. Thorndike's three major laws were these:

- The law of readiness

- The law of exercise

- The law of effect

The law of readiness states that the individual must be ready to act in order for the S-R bond to form. Unreadiness does not produce a response to the stimulus. This highlights the importance of having material and experiences appropriate to the level of group members. Motivation, maturity, and ability of group members combine to affect readiness, but the leader contributes by understanding these factors and taking them into account when planning group activities.

The law of exercise proposes that meaningful practice or exercise is necessary for retention. If the learned response is not repeated over time, the strength of the S-R bond is weakened or lost. Group leaders will want to make provisions for repeating new material. Members need to practice the new concept or skill if it is to be retained. One presentation is not enough, in most instances; material should be presented in a variety of ways throughout the life of the group.

The law of effect proposes that when the S-R bond has been made and the response is satisfying, the bond is strengthened. On the other hand, if the response is unsatisfying, the bond is weakened or extinguished. The law of effect can be used in two ways: to increase certain behaviors and to decrease others. Some understanding of what is satisfying to group members and what is not provides clues that can be used to select activities and provide focus.

Operant Conditioning

Skinner (1953) expanded the concepts of conditioning by introducing the *reinforcement schedule*, the process for *shaping*, and the idea of *operant* or *operant behavior*. In classical conditioning, the presentation of the reinforcer determines the response. *Reinforcement* is provided on every trial paired with the stimulus. In operant or instrumental conditioning, only correct responses are reinforced. Skinner demonstrated that schedules of reinforcement could produce correct responses, or strong S-R. Reinforcement schedules provided for variations in reinforcement and demonstrated that every correct response did not have to be reinforced for the response to be repeated or retained.

Reinforcers differ between individuals. What may be reinforcing to one person has no impact on another. However, a group leader can count on most members having a positive reaction to approval. A group leader can use this reinforcer by being accepting of input, verbalizing appreciation, and noting when members appear to be making special efforts.

Shaping, also called *successive approximation*, uses reinforcement to shape or mold desired behavior. Rather than waiting for the desired behavior to occur on its own, the leader encourages it by reinforcing successive steps to the final response or behavior. Many attitudes, customs, and learned goals are formed through shaping.

Shaping is accomplished over time and usually is not done consciously. Members' attitudes, beliefs, values, and some behaviors are results of shaping that has occurred throughout their lives. Systematic shaping cannot be accomplished in brief groups but contributions to shaping can take place. It is important for the group leader to understand that group members have been shaped as they are over time.

Operant behaviors and *operants* are those responses that manipulate or behave on the environment and are instrumental in achieving a reinforcer. These differ from respondent behaviors by acting to produce the directed stimulus instead of being affected by the stimulus that precedes the response. In simpler terms, the focus of attention is on the relationship of the individual and the environment. Individuals impact their environment, they are not at the whim or mercy of it.

There are six operant techniques:

- positive reinforcement

- extinction

- differential reinforcement

- response shaping

- punishment

- negative reinforcement

Some form of each of these techniques may have applications to psychoeducational groups; I encourage you to explore these concepts in more depth than they are presented here.

Mediation Stimulus-Response in Learning

Theorists such as Hull (1943), Mowrer (1960), Wolpe (1958), and Dollard and Miller (1950) have postulated that an organism's internal processes (i.e., the mediation, or the "O" in S-O-R theory) also interact with a stimulus to produce a response. Internal processes such as drives, emotional responses that have been previously learned, cognitions, and interferences of the new on the previously learned are mediations and are considered to be significant influences on learning.

Dollard and Miller (1950) summarized the S-O-R theory this way: Learning involves a drive or need for action; cues to provide information and direction to the response; the response; and the reinforcement. Wolpe (1958) expanded this view in his description of reciprocal inhibition, which holds that new responses inhibit, eliminate, or weaken old ones. Wolpe's learning theory gave counselors specific approaches—such as assertiveness training, systematic desensitization, and aversion therapy—for treating maladaptive behavior.

Assertiveness training helps clients learn to respond to others in ways that are neither submissive nor aggressive. Assertive responses reflect a healthy self-concept and high self-esteem while respecting the rights of others. Assertiveness training includes socials skills training, modeling, and behavioral rehearsal. Simulations, role-play, structured exercises, and relaxation training are some of the strategies and techniques associated with assertiveness training.

Systematic desensitization is a counter-condition technique designed to eliminate or change a habitual reaction to a stimulus. The three components of systematic desensitization are the construction of an anxiety hierarchy, relaxation, and scene presentation during relaxation.

Aversion therapy uses the principle of avoidance learning where an unpleasant, punishing stimulus is administered simultaneously with an emerging pleasurable response. The intent is to make the pleasurable response extinct or significantly reduced. Aversion therapy has been found to be effective in treating long-standing conditions such as obsessions.

Social Learning Theories

Social learning theories build on S-O-R theories by including environmental influences and cognitive processes interacting with behavior. Environmental influences or conditions are affected by people's actions, which then influence resulting behaviors (Bandura, 1977). Cognitive processes—attitudes, beliefs, values, and expectations—are internal and greatly influence how the environment and stimuli are experienced by an individual. Considerable weight is given to self-direction in social learning theories.

Kurt Lewin (1890-1947), E. C. Tolman (1886-1959), Albert Bandura (1977), and Julian Rotter (1959) are social learning theorists who can be described as *phenomenologists* because they consider an individual's interaction with the world to be personal, influenced by his or her perception or construction of the world.

Social learning theory emphasizes learning new adjustive responses, instead of merely eliminating old responses, and changing expectations and reinforcement values to provide satisfaction. Behavior is considered to be goal-directed. An important concept in this theory is that personality is an interaction of the individual and his or her self-constructed meaningful environment.

Insight Theories

Insight, field, or gestalt learning theories propose that learning happens as a result of modifications that occur in response to meaningful patterns or configurations. The learner reorganizes old learning to grasp new material. This reorganization involves transformation to produce new patterns and stabilization to produce consolidation of the new organizations. Relationships between the new and the old are critical.

Max Wertheimer (1880-1943), Kurt Koffka (1886-1941), and Wolfgang Koehler (1887-1961) conducted experiments on integrated perception—Wertheimer and Koffka focusing on movement, Koehler on visual perception in apes. They found that perception is affected by patterns and organization, and that the two changes constituting learning are perceptual and cognitive.

Gestalt is a German term that does not directly translate into English. The most common definition is this: "The whole is greater than the sum of its parts." This definition emphasizes holistic, patterning, organization, and field property concepts, whereby individuals tend to see "wholes" rather than discrete "parts," and figure takes precedence over ground. Insight is thought to be the instant grasping of the whole, of patterns, or of reorganizations.

According to insight theories, three conditions are necessary for learning: a goal, structure, and insight. In this scheme, behavior is goal-directed, structure refers to the individual's internal perceptions or way of organizing the world, and insight is the sudden coming together of previously unrelated components to form a whole that can be understood.

BASIC PRINCIPLES OF LEARNING

There are several factors that affect the process of learning, including individual factors, methods, meaningfulness of material, transfer of learning, and retention. In the sections that follow, we'll look at each of these factors in turn.

Individual Factors

Intelligence, age, previous learning, motivation, and anxiety are some primary individual factors that influence the learning process.

Intelligence level is a combination of innate and acquired competencies. Worchel and Shebilske (1992) defined intelligence as "the capacity to learn and use information." There are many theories of intelligence, and I encourage you to explore them further.

Age and maturation also play a role in learning. Individuals cannot learn before they are ready to do so, and the interaction of age and maturation contribute to readiness. Learning also is hierarchical in nature; that is, knowledge builds upon previous learning and is interrelated. Some readiness for learning relates to motivation, but some (especially for children) is dependent on age and maturation.

Education level contributes much to learning. How much one has already learned relates significantly to one's ease and speed in learning new material, particularly if the new material relates in some way to the material previously learned. For example, learning applications is easier if principles have already been learned.

Motivation to learn is a complex and abstract concept. Maslow (1943) and Murray (1938) proposed "needs" as motivating influences. For Murray, *needs* were psychological in nature, such as the need for achievement. Maslow organized needs into a hierarchical system, beginning with basic physiological needs (such as food, water, sleep, and oxygen) and progressing to self-actualization needs (the desire for self-fulfillment). Other motivators include drive determinants, goal seeking, interests, incentives, and reinforcements.

The level of anxiety experienced by an individual also influences his or her learning. Fear of failure, lack of self-confidence, degree of self-efficacy, and their reversed counterparts (e.g., anticipation of success, self-confidence, etc.) affect the ability of the individual to learn. It is not always possible to determine which response will be elicited by anxiety. For example, fear of failure may elicit a response of hopelessness resulting in an unwillingness to try to learn new material. Or, someone who fears failure may have a reverse response where they try harder so that they will not fail. Previous experiences of success or failure can be projected onto new situations, which influences how the individual responds and is able to learn. Emotions experienced during a particular learning experience also are important determinants of outcomes.

Methods

The presentation of material also is important in learning. Even with the large variations in individual ability and willingness to learn, there are optimum methods that enhance the effectiveness and efficiency of learning for most people. These methods also influence retention, recall, and transfer. Among the major methods are active participation, distribution of practice, knowledge of results, and whole versus part.

Active participation enhances people's ability to learn. This appears to be true for cognitive as well as psychomotor tasks. Taking an active role promotes better understanding, retention, skill development, and applications. Paying attention, thinking about presented material, searching for patterns and relationships, asking questions, making comments, and practicing skills are examples of active participation.

Distribution of practice is another important factor. Learning, particularly learning a skill, is more effective if practice time is sufficiently long and is arranged so that there is continuity between cue and response and between response and reinforcement. When teaching skills, sequencing tasks, having frequent practice sessions, and emphasizing speed over accuracy are all important.

Knowledge of results (i.e., feedback) also is an important component of learning. The learner is encouraged when he or she receives input. The input can be either to affirm correctness or to identify and correct errors. Knowing how one is doing can increase one's time on-task, thereby increasing learning.

Whole versus part refers to seeing how the part fits into the whole. Although one must learn discrete units in order to know the whole (as one must learn the keyboard and commands in order to use a software program), learners do better when they are presented with the whole before dealing with the discrete units. Orienting and reviewing the entire task allows them to better understand how each discrete unit fits and its utility. Breaking a task down into manageable units allows learners to focus, to avoid feeling overwhelmed, and to deal with one thing at a time.

Meaningfulness of Material

Learners are motivated to learn and participate if the material has meaning for them. Students retain and understand material better when the material has significant associations for them. Associations with previously learned material, with internal needs or drives, or with emotional content contribute to meaningfulness for the learner.

Organizing material into conceptual categories can help the learner to see significant associations, particularly with previously learned materials. Humans appear to favor patterns and relationships, so it is helpful for their learning if the presenter takes time to ensure the meaningfulness of the material.

Transfer of Learning

Gagné (1965) described two types of learning transfer: horizontal and vertical. *Horizontal transfer* occurs when the learner can perform a new task at about the same level of difficulty as an old task. *Vertical transfer* takes place when old concepts or learning are used to learn or understand more complex concepts.

There are four major theories on transfer: formal discipline, identical elements, generalization, and transposition.

Formal Discipline Theory.   The classical curriculum of the nineteenth century was built on the idea that one should study Latin, Greek, logic, and mathematics because of their value in training the mind. For example, scholars held that the study of mathematics quickens the mental faculties so that they can meet any and all mental tasks. The real value of a subject, according to this theory, is that it is difficult: The study of difficult subjects strengthens the mind just as exercise strengthens the body. However, James (1890) demonstrated that practice in memorizing did not improve memory.

Theory of Identical Elements.   According to this theory, transfer can occur from one learning to another only so far as the two functions have elements in common. As the similarity decreases, there usually is a falling off in the amount of transfer. An application for this in psychoeducational groups is to highlight similarities between what is known (or previous experiences) and the new material introduced.

Generalization Theory. Judd (1908) emphasized that learning principles and meanings led to superior applications; that is, the principle learned in one situation could be applied to the performance of a task in a different situation. Leaders of psychoeducational groups can make use of this theory by providing numerous examples of applications for material and by soliciting possible examples from group members.

Transposition Theory (Gestalt). Also called *patterns of experience* (Wertheimer, 1959), this is the process of using the understanding of the inner structure of a problem to help deal with variations of the problem later. According to this theory, the learner responds as a unified and integrated organism to the total stimulus, using the following process.

1. A new problem is perceived as a whole with parts, as is the previous situation, which is deemed to have similarities to the new problem.

2. Similarities between the old and new sub-parts are considered without losing sight of the whole.

3. The inner structures of the old and the new are examined to determine how they are interrelated.

4. An understanding of the similarities and inner structure emerge that also aid in dealing with other variations of the situation that may present in the future.

5. The entire process is a consistent line of thinking with constant reference to the whole.

The primary emphases for transposition theory are the constant and consistent reference to the whole problem situation, the interrelatedness of essential sub-parts for the old and the new, and the understandings that result to help recognize variations that occur in the future.

Retention

Material not only must be learned, it must be retained if it is to be of use to the learner. Retention is influenced by several factors and can best be understood by looking at what and why people forget.

Studies conducted by Ebbinhaus (1885, as cited in Garrison & Magoon, 1972) provided considerable information on forgetting and retention, and those findings are still relevant today. The most important of Ebbinhaus's findings was that there is a tendency to quickly forget material that has little or no meaning for the learner. Material with high meaningfulness may be retained indefinitely with little or no forgetting.

There are two primary theories of forgetting: trace-decay and interference. *Trace decay theory* proposes that traces of memory not used will gradually fade away, while traces of memory that are used will be strengthened and retained.

Interference theory posits two causes of forgetting: proactive and retroactive inhibition. *Proactive inhibition* occurs when previous learning gets in the way of learning new material. *Retroactive inhibition* occurs when new information gets in the way of retrieving old information.

Rate and Extent of Forgetting. The rate of forgetting is a function of the degree to which the material was learned in the first place, the relevance of learning to the learner's needs, intervening influences, actions connected to the material following the learning, and the physical and psychological state of the individual both at learning and at recall. These factors interact and are interrelated, and the degree and extent to which they do so may differ between individuals. Material is more likely to be retained if these conditions are met:

1. It was thoroughly learned in the first place.

2. It has meaning for the learner.

3. Intervening situations, circumstances, or actions are not strong or traumatic enough to interfere.

4. The material is used in some way after being learned.

5. The learner is physically and psychologically able to learn and to retrieve the material.

The extent of forgetting sometimes is called the *curve of forgetting* (Ebbinhaus, 1885, as cited in Garrison & Magoon, 1972), describing how much of newly learned material is forgotten immediately after learning and how the part that is remembered is retained over time. Five factors influence the curve of forgetting: learned material is not used, retroactive inhibition, proactive inhibition, reorganization of knowledge, and psychological factors.

1. The principle of *use it or lose it* appears to hold true for retaining learned material. Use of material can refer to practice or to review.

2. Retroactive inhibition (new information interfering with old) does not just refer to new information about the subject under discussion, such as learning new theories of counseling. It also refers to moving from topic to topic when there is little or no relationship between topics (e.g., learning new material in mathematics and then learning new material in history). Some of both are retained, but much of both is forgotten.

3. Proactive inhibition can be seen in those not willing or not able to let new information in. Unlearning of and modifications to what has been learned before appear to be difficult.

4. Humans are attracted to patterns and relationships. Even when these are not apparent, the human mind seeks them or reorganizes material so that they appear. Newly learned material is reorganized to fit with familiar concepts or objects. When new material cannot be reorganized to fit, it is less easily retained. If patterns or relationships are not apparent to the individual, little may be retained.

5. Resistances and defenses also play a role in forgetting. People may have unconscious defense mechanisms against threatening or uncomfortable material. For example, individuals who lack confidence in their mathematics ability or who have a lot of anxiety around mathematics may unconsciously block mathematics material, either not learning it or easily forgetting it.

PRINCIPLES OF INSTRUCTION FOR PSYCHOEDUCATIONAL GROUPS

Learning theories provide a framework for determining principles to guide instruction for psychoeducational groups. The same principles relate to instruction in more formal settings, but they are used somewhat differently for psychoeducational groups. Knowing how people learn, retain, and transfer material can help the leader develop strategies for presenting information in a group.

The educational component for most psychoeducational groups is significant; in fact, it typically is the one most emphasized. Teaching participants

TABLE 2.2
Principles and Tasks

Principle of Instruction	Leader Task(s)
Clear goals	Develop reasonable goals; Review goals with participants; Obtain commitment to goals from participants
Readiness	Understand educational, maturity and age levels of participants; Develop goals, etc. based on participant's levels
Motivation	Understand the role of personal needs, etc. in motivation; Plan activities to meet needs; Review activities with participants and incorporate suggestions
Active vs. passive	Provide for participant's active involvement; Use experiential activities, games, simulations, etc.; Encourage questions and discussion
Organization	Plan for new material to be associated with previously learned material; Present whole before part; Organize presentation to be hierarchical; Material should be meaningful
Comprehension	Make significant connections of materials to participants; Illustrate significance, meanings, implications, and applications
Practice	Provide opportunities for repetition, review, etc.

specific information, strategies, and skills are primary goals in most groups, so developing instructional strategies to maximize learning is a major task for the leader.

Table 2.2 presents the primary principles and leader tasks in psychoeducational groups. Each principle will be discussed briefly in the following sections.

Goals

The leader of a psychoeducational group usually develops the goals for the group, particularly for the educational component. These goals should be specific, clear, direct, and unambiguous. They should be developed with the needs, readiness, and motivations of participants in mind. This may be somewhat difficult, as the leader may know little or nothing of the participants as individuals prior to the first group meeting. However, the leader will know some general things that can provide suggestions about the learners' characteristics. For example, if the group is focused on time management for engineers, the participants are most likely to be college-educated, over 21, and male.

In addition to developing clear goals, the leader must review these goals with participants and get agreement to work toward them. The leader should review the goals with participants at the beginning of the session and ask if they seem appropriate, what changes they might suggest, and if they can agree to work toward them. For groups with involuntary members, the leader may decide to have participants sign a contract to work on the goals. This has been shown to be particularly effective with children and adolescents.

Readiness

The lack of knowledge about participants makes this factor difficult for the leader. Members usually are not prescreened, and the leader typically is not provided records or background data for most groups. Exceptions may be involuntary participants for some groups (such as those focused on anger control).

However, the leader usually knows some general characteristics of members from which he or she can draw inferences about the readiness of participants for certain activities. For example, in preparing an adolescent social skills training group for boys the leader can reasonably infer that the members lack certain skills, will likely be either silent or very active because of embarrassment or anxiety, may not have volunteered for the group, may be wary and suspicious of authority figures, and may lack maturity for their age. The leader of such a group might need to address safety and trust issues, "sell" members on participating, and present material more slowly.

Motivation

Motivation may be external (i.e., in the form of a reward) or internal (i.e., by satisfying a need). Generally, the leader can expect that members will have or need both kinds of motivation. If the psychoeducational group does not provide mechanisms for achieving both or either, the leader will find the group difficult, and little or no learning will take place.

Since there usually is no pregroup interviewing, the leader typically does not have the opportunity to get input on participants' motivators. Some may be evident, such as the wish to avoid incarceration. Others, such as a need for achievement, are internal processes that must be inferred from behavior over time or by self-report.

The leader can make accommodations to provide motivators or to encourage group members' self-motivation. Planning activities to encourage participation by motivating is the first step. Younger participants typically respond to tangible rewards (for example, candy). Older participants like tangible rewards as well, but they also want to know what participation will do for them. A motivator may be provided by outside forces, such as an employer. Accessing internal motivators is somewhat more difficult. One thing the leader can do is to review the proposed schedule and activities and obtain input from participants on how well the planned activities meet their individual needs, request additional suggestions and incorporate them, or allow participants to help set the agenda.

The most important step a leader can take is to understand the developmental levels of participants, the background of the condition (such as anger and violence), strategies generally found to be successful, and the role of motivation in learning. Reading the literature can provide some needed information.

Active Versus Passive

Active involvement enhances learning. Hands-on activities promote "learning by doing." Active participation includes group members responding in a discussion, role-playing, drawing, writing, talking, and engaging in movement. Less learning takes place with passive participation, for example, by listening to a lecture.

The leader has more control over this factor than over most others. He or she is responsible for planning and designing the learning experiences, which provides the opportunity to ensure that the activities encourage active participation.

Another responsibility of the leader is to encourage questions and discussion. The section on questioning under "Developing Skills" (in chapter 3) gives more information on how to use questioning effectively, and on how to respond to questions from participants.

Organization

It is essential that the material being presented is organized in such a way that it is meaningful, can be associated with previous learning, is hierarchical, and is appropriate for the allotted time. Careful thought and planning promote good organization.

Organizing materials for a largely unknown audience is not easy. Even when the leader has relevant information about participants, organizing is not an easy task. Most leaders overprepare and have more materials and activities than can be covered in the available time. This is preferred to underpreparing, however, because it is much easier to discard material than to stretch material out. There also are groups that, for unknown or unanticipated reasons, will explore topics or activities in more depth. A leader is well advised not to truncate the extended exploration *if it is beneficial*. If members appear to be getting more out of the in-depth exploration than they would be out of the next planned topic or activity, this is reason enough to stick with it.

Another aspect of organization for psychoeducational groups is to keep it moving. Transition from one activity to the next should occur before boredom and disinterest appear. There must be adequate time to process activities, but you should not linger over a topic too long.

A good sequence to follow in a group session is a short lecture or presentation; questions and discussion; exercise, role-play, game, or simulation; processing of activity, and summarization. Even a short one time session can repeat the sequence. For additional information, see the section on "Taxonomy" below.

Comprehension

The leader should provide many examples, illustrations, and descriptions for concepts and other significant material. These help participants learn through association and repetition. Often, the leader does not know participants' comprehension needs and levels. Giving examples helps increase the probability of making significant connections for most participants.

When applications are important, it is helpful to have several illustrations or examples. It also is helpful if participants can provide additional examples or make suggestions. The most important thing to remember is that meaningfulness of material promotes and enhances learning.

Taxonomy

Bloom, Krathwohl, and Masia (1956) developed the cognitive domain for the *Taxonomy of Educational Objectives,* which is useful for establishing instructional goals. These are hierarchical and provide a framework for sequencing and organizing material. The cognitive domain has six levels that call for thinking to move from simple to complex.

1. **Knowledge.** The first level includes cognitive activity focused on recall of specifics, universals, methods, processes, patterns, facts, terminology, trends, principles, and generalizations. Some implications for the leader of a psychoeducational group include these: Be sure to define terms even if you believe that participants are familiar with them; be specific about principles, concepts, and so on that are part of the presentation; and be cautious in making assumptions about what participants already know.

2. **Comprehension.** The second level incorporates and extends knowledge to include interpretation, translation, and extrapolation. Leaders can use this level to get feedback from participants about their levels of understanding. This also gives an opportunity to fill in missing information and to correct misunderstandings and faulty knowledge.

3. **Application.** Level 3 provides for selective use of abstractions (formed from knowledge and understandings) in particular situations. The leader presents applications after presenting facts and giving feedback on the participants' understanding of the facts. Participants who can suggest appropriate applications are demonstrating successful completion of levels 1 and 2.

4. **Analysis.** Level 4 cognitive processes include the ability to see discrete elements as well a the whole. Analyzing relationships, patterns, and organizing principles are examples of this. This level involves a relatively high degree of knowledge and experience with the topic, so the leader may be the only one at this level.

5. **Synthesis.** Level 5 incorporates the previous four levels together with the creation of a different or new perspective, product, or process. This level of learning would be somewhat unusual for the purposes or goals of most psychoeducational groups. Groups that have a problem-solving focus may achieve this level. Groups that have personal

issue involvement as a primary component may see some members reach this level, especially if the group runs for several sessions.

6. **Evaluation.** Although this is considered the highest level for cognitive processes, evaluation can interact with all of the other levels. It is defined as making judgments about strengths and weaknesses, positive and negative points, adequacy and inadequacies. The interaction with other levels can help increase accomplishments at those levels. For example, evaluating the adequacy of knowledge on a particular topic can lead to more in-depth information being sought or given.

TECHNIQUES

Psychoeducational groups employ a variety of formats, making it difficult to name a specific set of techniques applicable to all. The variety of participants and their characteristics and the range of educational emphases provide additional confounding variables. Therefore, the techniques described here are not necessarily the "preferred methods," but they give a sense of the variety of techniques that can be used.

Lectures

To be effective, lectures should be well-organized presentations that lead the listener from point to point to provide an integrated knowledge and understanding of the material. Lectures are efficient ways of getting across a large amount of information in a short time. However, lectures have several drawbacks, including these:

Listeners tend to have short attention spans unless the topic and presentation grab and hold their interest.

Listening to a lecture is a passive form of learning, which is less effective than active forms.

Lecturing demands considerable planning, organizing, and presenting on the part of the leader.

If a leader plans to use lectures as part of a psychoeducational group, he or she should use mini-lectures, lasting no more than 20 minutes, instead. These are most effective if kept to 10 or 15 minutes. Members are more inclined to listen for that period than for a longer span. Further, having several mini-lectures interspersed with activities to reinforce the material will lead to more learning and retention. The leader also should restrict the amount of material to that which members can use.

Discussion

This technique can be used to promote active involvement. Lively discussions contribute interest to the session and encourage participants to be involved. Discussion as a technique can be differentiated from discussion groups, where the main purpose is to engage in discussing. As a technique, discussion is not the goal of the group; it is typically kept short, so that other activities can happen. Fewer member may be involved, and members tend to talk to the leader rather than to each other.

Leaders can initiate discussion by asking questions, by calling for comments or questions, and by encouraging exploration of points, issues, or concepts. The exchange of ideas, opinions, and experiences can be energizing to the group. Members feel their input is valued and that they have something to contribute.

Exercises and Games

Exercises, games, simulations, and role-play are all forms of experiential learning. These are designed to produce more active involvement on the part of participants, to focus on and emphasize a particular point, and to provide an opportunity for affective as well as cognitive learning.

Experiential groups constitute a major category of psychoeducational groups, and there is some overlap with skills training. When exercises or other forms of experiential learning are used, members can integrate affective and cognitive learning, which contributes to and intensifies retention.

Several specific strategies should be employed to ensure safety for group participants, since experiential learning can arouse unexpected and uncomfortable feelings. The leader must have the expertise to help members deal with these feelings, which can be intense, and to plan sessions so that the likelihood of these intense, uncomfortable feelings being aroused is minimized.

Exercises and games can be fun as well as educational. When learning is enjoyable, motivation is increased, comprehension is enhanced, and retention is promoted. Planning, conducting, and processing experiential group activities are discussed more fully in the section titled "Planning Experiential Group Activities" in chapter 8.

Media

Movies, audio and video tapes, computer presentations, and slides are examples of media. Media cover a large amount of material in a short time. They also have an advantage as they tend to capture interest more easily, can provide visual illustrations of material, and have been demonstrated to be effective in learning.

The primary disadvantage of media is that they do not actually involve the learner. (The exception may be computers, but that still depends on what is being presented via the computer and if the learner is expected to interact with the machine.)

The leader of psychoeducational groups should make judicious use of media. Used as accents or lead-ins, media presentations can be quite effective. Used too frequently or for too long a time, however, media presentations are ineffective. Timing is important as well: Having participants passively watch a video immediately after lunch, for example, is more likely to induce sleep than to promote learning. Plan for media to be an enhancement, not the primary technique.

Use of Techniques

The leader of psychoeducational groups can use several different techniques that will be effective. Experience promotes understanding of when to use what with whom, and expected outcomes. Using these techniques to their best effect is a major thrust of this book, but the most effective group leaders also learn from their own experiences.

Chapter 3

THE LEADER

The most effective leaders of psychoeducational groups possess certain characteristics and skills—characteristics being "what you are" and skills, "what you can do." Some of these characteristics can be developed, but they must be internalized and become an integral part of your personality in order to be effective. Skills can be more easily taught, although they may not be easy to learn or to master.

BASIC CHARACTERISTICS

Major characteristics of an effective group leader include these:

- A belief in the group process

- Confidence in oneself and in one's ability

- The courage to risk

- A willingness to admit one's mistakes and imperfections

- A facility for organizing and planning

- Flexibility

- The ability to tolerate ambiguity

- Self-awareness

- A sense of humor

Other characteristics that are helpful are those you would need for leading counseling or therapy groups, including caring, warmth, positive regard, and genuineness.

Belief in the Group Process

A leader's belief in the group process provides an atmosphere of safety for group members. While the issues may not be openly addressed, many members of psychoeducational groups have the same safety and trust issues as do members of counseling or therapy groups: They wonder if the group will be of any benefit to them, if they will be accepted and respected, and if the leader can take care of them. Leaders who have a deeply held belief in the efficacy of the group provide reassurance to these members on a subconscious level, that their participation in the group will be of personal benefit. This reassurance is conveyed in the preplanning the leader does, in how members are prepared for group, in how their spoken and unspoken questions are addressed, and in the leader's flexibility.

Self-Confidence

Confidence in oneself and in one's ability is almost self-explanatory. The leader who models self-confidence teaches group members by example. Developing self-confidence happens over time through positive experiences; that is, the quality of your experiences affect your acceptance of your ability. For some, positive experiences include approval and praise from others. While everyone needs some feedback on how they are perceived or on how well they have learned to do something, some people gain more confidence when there is consistent, positive feedback from many others; this is one of the things that can happen in a group. Confidence also is enhanced when a member tries out a new skill and the desired results occur. Again, it must be noted that confidence develops over time. Confidence in your group leadership skills also develops over time with appropriate feedback.

The Courage to Risk

Taking a risk means being willing to expose yourself to possible failure or to criticism from others, being willing to seek new experiences, to be in error, to grow, and to develop. An effective group leader is dynamic—always growing, always changing. While he or she may be teaching the same content to many different groups, the leader should always be a searching for better methods, more participant learning, and so on. Risk-taking also comes into play during sessions. Leaders need not be perfect, and sessions sometimes can be enhanced if the leader will take a risk.

The Ability to Admit Mistakes

A willingness to admit mistakes and imperfections can be helpful under certain conditions. By admitting mistakes, the leader models an acceptance of self and conveys an attitude of acceptance of others. In other words, if you can show that you accept yourself and own your mistakes and imperfections, group members can believe that you will accept them and not expect them to be perfect. This does *not* mean that apologies are always needed; it simply means that you should own and take responsibility for your own errors or imperfections without denigrating yourself, feeling shame, or turning on others and blaming or criticizing.

Being Organized

Being organized and having a "planful" nature constitutes a hybrid of characteristic and skill. It is possible to teach organizational and planning skills, but the desire for organizing and planning is an internal one. Effective leaders do considerable work before group sessions to ensure the efficacy of the group for members. Planning and organizing help ensure the safety of members, promote participation, reduce anxiety for the leader and for members, and enhance learning. How to plan and organize is addressed more extensively in the section on "Pregroup Preparation" in chapter 7.

Flexibility

Flexibility is a result of confidence and the ability to tolerate your own and others' anxiety. The willingness to change a planned process or activity is not something that can be taught, but it is a characteristic of confident group leaders. The ability to look at a changing situation and make appropriate adjustments can facilitate the progress of the group. When the group leader lacks flexibility, members may feel stifled, controlled, and overdirected. The flip side is that too much flexibility promotes anxiety, as members are unable to judge what is expected or what will happen next. Striking the proper balance is a learned trait or skill.

Tolerance of Ambiguity

In planning a group, it is useful to know things like educational level, abilities, emotional concerns, and physical conditions of members. However, since many psychoeducational groups do not allow for prescreening, leaders often do not know much about members prior to the first session, and so must prepare in a vacuum. Furthermore, some groups have involuntary membership—that is, members do not choose to participate—and *the leader may not even know it*. Leaders who feel comfortable and confident in the face of knowing little about members are better able to conduct effective groups.

Self-Awareness

Self-awareness is an ongoing developmental process. It is an important characteristic for leaders of all types of groups. Countertransference issues arise even in psychoeducational groups, and the effective leader knows enough to be aware of personal issues, recognize countertransference when it appears, and understand its impact on the group and on members.

Personal ownership of attitudes, behaviors, opinions, and feelings is both a characteristic and a skill. Ownership is a characteristic because it is basically internalized. In order to genuinely take responsibility for your attitudes, behaviors, opinions, and feelings, you must accept that they are yours and are not imposed on you by others. Feeling that someone else has provoked any or all of these characteristics means you are not accepting ownership of them. Mere lip service to assuming ownership is not enough, it has to come from within.

In addition to being a characteristic, there is also a skill component: that of conveying to others that you accept personal ownership. Another aspect is respect and toleration of differing points of view. Skill in conveying your attitudes, opinions, and feelings in such a way that others do not feel compelled to adopt them is one you should develop. Members will be turned off if you come across as dogmatic and as having all the right answers. While members are attending the group to learn, they are not blank slates on which you can write.

A Sense of Humor

A sense of humor allows the leader to take him- or herself less seriously and models for members the ability to see the humorous side of a situation. People who can laugh at themselves usually are healthier than those who cannot. Additionally, seeing the humor in something relieves tension, promotes a sense of playfulness, and contributes to a general sense of well-being.

Core Characteristics

The usefulness of core therapeutic characteristics—that is, caring, warmth, positive regard, and genuineness—has been well-documented. While there are nonverbal behaviors that convey these characteristics, it is difficult to fake them; they must come from within and are an integral part of one's being. Even in psychoeducational groups, the leader needs to have these characteristics, as they tend to promote learning, the goal for these groups.

Caring is shown through attending, listening, and directly responding. Physically orienting yourself to the speaker, maintaining eye contact, and hearing the meaning (not just the words) all convey caring to the speaker.

Warmth is shown through some of the same behaviors, but adds a facial expression of concern for the other person. Smiles or other appropriate facial expressions convey warmth.

Positive regard means being open to the speaker and willing to hear his or her point of view without judging the person to be good or bad because that viewpoint is different from yours. Positive regard assumes the worth and uniqueness of the other.

Genuineness (or authenticity) is being willing to let yourself be known to the other *as you really are*: no false pretenses; no reluctance to share thoughts, opinions, or feelings; and a real appreciation of the other as he or she presents him- or herself to you.

GROUP LEADERSHIP SKILLS

Leading psychoeducational groups requires some basic counseling skills, including these:

- attending,
- reflecting,
- summarizing,

- active listening and responding,
- clarifying, and
- supporting.

In addition, the leader needs some advanced counseling skills, including linking, blocking, tuning in to process, confronting, and terminating.

All of these are important and may be used in other than traditional ways. With practice, these can become an integral part of your skill set. These skills are described below, and suggested strategies for developing them are given in the section titled "Developing Skills" later in this chapter.

Attending

Preparation to listen, respect for others, and interest in others are conveyed by attending skills. These are primarily nonverbal behaviors, such as a slight forward lean, eye contact, orientation of the body toward the speaker, and not allowing yourself to be distracted from the speaker. Attending to members when they are speaking makes them feel valued and that there is interest in what they have to say.

Active Listening and Responding

Active listening and responding means being able to hear and understand direct and indirect communications and to convey your understanding to the other person. Tuning in to feelings, hearing the metacommunication, and understanding the role of nonverbal behaviors in communication all play important roles in active listening and responding. Self-awareness is important to the extent that you understand your personal issues and how they may affect your listening and responding skills.

Reflecting

Reflection is a useful skill with psychoeducational groups because members do not always say what they mean, and leaders don't always understand what they means. Reflecting back what was heard allows both to correct any misunderstandings and can produce further elaborations.

Clarifying

Clarification goes along with reflection and active listening. This is the skill of understanding what was meant, illuminating intent, clearing up misconceptions and misunderstandings, and providing clearer direction.

Summarizing

Summarizing the key elements of a session helps members tie the many parts of the experience together. Sessions usually begin with objectives. Summaries show how or if the objectives were met, remaining questions or concerns, other emerging issues, and some qualitative judgments about the session. So much has transpired that members may have forgotten what they set out to do, and the summary reminds them that they accomplished the objective(s).

Supporting

Supporting by the group leader must be done with care. You must not rush in to provide support, but instead should judge when members need support and when they can be left to work it out on their own. Learning when support will be productive, and when it is counterproductive, comes with experience.

Advanced Skills

There is a category of group leadership skills that is difficult to label. These are the advanced skills of linking, blocking, tuning in to process, confronting, and terminating. These skills are more complicated, making them difficult to define, describe, and develop. Each skill is briefly described here. Confronting is discussed in greater depth in chapter 6.

> **Linking** involves relating what members are doing and saying among the group. Seeing and pointing out commonalities, similarities, and patterns is an advanced skill that comes with practice and experience. The leader has to really listen to discern such commonalities and patterns. Illuminating them promotes growth and development for the group and for individual members: The group can become more cohesive, and members can relate to each other in meaningful ways and gain in self-awareness. Linking is useful for psychoeducational and for counseling/therapy groups.

> **Blocking** involves intervening to stop intellectualizing, storytelling, inappropriate responses, or any behavior that negatively affects the progress of the group or the well-being of group members. Blocking must be done so that it cuts off the undesired behavior without blaming or criticizing. You must take care not to make members feel chastised or wrong. While such inappropriate behaviors can and do occur

in psychoeducational groups, they are more likely to appear in counseling/therapy groups.

Tuning in to process involves evaluating the ongoing progress and process of the group, which generally is left to the leader. Most of the other skills discussed here can be manifested by group members, but evaluation requires a knowledge of group process generally not held by members unless they have had education or training in it. Understanding the stages of a group and the process taking place in it are skills developed by the experienced group leader.

Confronting is a skill that is misunderstood by many people. It has come to be synonymous with attack. The accurate meaning of confrontation, however, does not involve attacking, telling someone off, or force of any kind. Confrontation is an invitation, not an imposition. The receiver is invited to look at an aspect of him- or herself and its impact on others. Confrontation is extended tentatively, not forced on the other person. Telling someone what you think they need to know is an attack, not a confrontation. The giver of the confrontation must be clear about her or her personal motives for the confrontation before embarking upon one. Wanting to retaliate, tell someone off, or discount another person are inappropriate reasons for confronting. Guidelines for constructive confrontation are discussed in chapter 6.

Terminating: It is important to have constructive endings for sessions. Too many times experiences are simply stopped, not ended in such a way as to provide closure for participants. You should take time to decisively end sessions. Constructive termination ensures that loose ends are tied up, important and intense feelings are dealt with so members are not left dangling, and participants have an opportunity to say good-bye to one another.

Knowing what is effective and what to avoid is important for group leaders. Many of these skills seem relatively easy to master *in isolation*. It is much more difficult to use them when so much is happening in the group at every moment. All groups are dynamic, and the effective leader recognizes and accepts that fact and does not attempt to ignore the complexity.

Further, an effective leader is aware of his or her personal needs and uses these in constructive ways to facilitate the group. Group members are valued as worthwhile, unique individuals and not as pawns to be manipulated for their own or for the leader's good.

DEVELOPING SKILLS

Many group leadership skills can be described and easily understood. Others are more complex, and even their descriptions may not do them justice. Some examples of the more complex leadership skills are linking, blocking and summarizing.

Basic communication skills form the foundation for group leadership skills. The leader must be able to attend, paraphrase, and reflect as a part of active listening and responding; question appropriately; and confront in a constructive way. These skills allow the leader to be facilitative and to structure and perform those task and relationship functions that help groups progress and be successful. Further, these basic skills are the foundation on which more complex skills are developed. The leader calls on all of the basic skills to link, block, and summarize.

Elements of Effective Communication

A leader is more effective if he or she uses clear, concise, direct, and open communication. The effective leader takes steps to ensure that he or she understands and is understood. Some characteristics of effective communication are two-way active listening, feedback, lack of listener stress, clarity, and focusing on the core issue.

Two-Way Communication. Two-way communication means that ideas, information, opinions, attitudes, and feelings flow between communicators. For psychoeducational groups, this means that the leader and members each contribute to the functioning of the group. An effective leader uses the resources in the group, as well as his or her own knowledge and expertise, to attain the goals of the group. You should never assume that members have little or nothing to contribute. While the leader is, or should be, more knowledgeable, members need to feel competent also.

Active Listening. Active listening cannot be overemphasized. Hearing what was said and understanding what was meant are skills an effective leader must develop. Messages involve both feelings and content, but most listening focuses only on content, with little attention to feelings. This is a critical mistake, as the primary part of the message is the feeling part—not the content. Because psychoeducational groups usually are content- and task-oriented, the focus tends to be on those aspects, and feelings often are overlooked or discounted. No matter how important content is, the metacommunication of feelings is important to hear and respond to.

Effective Feedback. Effective feedback has several components: active listening and responding, attention to nonverbal behaviors, realizing the impact of the feedback on the other person, and the amount and timing of feedback. Feedback is effective when the receiver can absorb and use it. It is ineffective if the receiver feels overwhelmed or attacked, rejects or resists the feedback, or has an undesirable reaction to it (e.g., withdrawal). As leader, you should give only the amount of feedback a receiver can tolerate or use, not the amount you wish to give him or her. Specific guidelines for this are given in the section on "Developing Skills" later in this chapter.

Lack of Listener Stress. Lack of stress refers to communicating without having to worry that one is understood. This means the leader uses vocabulary appropriate for the audience, concepts that are generally understood and jargon-free, and limited amounts of information. Nothing is more disagreeable to group members than to feel the leader is "talking down" to them. Effective leaders gauge the comprehension level of participants and communicate in terms that promote interactions and understanding. As leader, you have enough variables to consider without worrying if members understand what you mean.

Clarity. It is not possible to have all communication be clear and unambiguous. However, effective communication strives for that ideal. This is particularly important in groups in which considerable activity is taking place and intense feelings are apt to be present at any time. One problem encountered is that everyone tends to hear or understand through a perceptual filter; that is, one's past experiences, relationships, sense of self, and level of emotionality interact to filter what is heard and understood. In some instances, the perceptual filter distorts what is communicated. You can help by clarifying what was said or what was meant.

Focusing on the Core Issue. Focusing on the core issue is a complex skill that incorporates active listening, linking, summarizing, and an understanding of issues and the indirect ways they may be communicated. This skill is learned over time.

Tables 3.1 and 3.2 are designed to help you become aware of your listening habits and communication style. You may find it helpful to record your answers to the scales and to ask someone with whom you interact on a regular basis to rate you as well. The items also provide a list of behaviors you might want to increase, decrease, or eliminate.

TABLE 3.1
Listening Habits Scale

Directions: Rate the frequency with which you do the following.

Listening	Frequency				
	Almost Always	Usually	Some-times	Seldom	Almost Never
1. Calling the subject uninteresting:	___	___	___	___	___
2. Criticizing the speaker's delivery or mannerisms:	___	___	___	___	___
3. Getting overstimulated by something the speaker says:	___	___	___	___	___
4. Listening primarily for facts:	___	___	___	___	___
5. Trying to outline everything:	___	___	___	___	___
6. Faking attention to the speaker:	___	___	___	___	___
7. Allowing interfering distractions:	___	___	___	___	___
8. Avoiding difficult material:	___	___	___	___	___
9. Letting emotion-laden words arouse personal antagonism:	___	___	___	___	___
10. Wasting the advantage of thought speed (daydreaming):	___	___	___	___	___
11. Interrupting the speaker:	___	___	___	___	___
12. Becoming distracted by others:	___	___	___	___	___

TABLE 3.2
Effective Verbal Communication Behavior

Directions: Rate yourself on the items below using the following scale:

5 = I do this most of the time or all of the time.
4 = I do this often.
3 = I do this sometimes; more often than not.
2 = I seldom do this.
1 = I do this little or none at all.

1.	Restate what others say without parroting	5	4	3	2	1
2.	Restate what others say without adding to the meaning	5	4	3	2	1
3.	Make clearer what others mean in what they say	5	4	3	2	1
4.	Check with others to ensure clear understanding	5	4	3	2	1
5.	Focus on underlying feelings	5	4	3	2	1
6.	Focus on underlying issues	5	4	3	2	1
7.	Bring conflicting thoughts/feelings into focus	5	4	3	2	1
8.	Identify commonalities between self and others	5	4	3	2	1
9.	Combine, tie together or identify themes in verbal interactions	5	4	3	2	1
10.	Ask questions only for information, not to get my point across	5	4	3	2	1
11.	Seek not to bombard others with questions	5	4	3	2	1
12.	Make more statements than questions in conversations	5	4	3	2	1
13.	Focus my questions on "what" and "how," rather than on "why"	5	4	3	2	1
14.	Allow others to express difficult feelings without interrupting	5	4	3	2	1
15.	Let others interpret their behavior	5	4	3	2	1
16.	Reflect feelings accurately	5	4	3	2	1
17.	Sense what feelings others are trying to express	5	4	3	2	1
18.	Refrain from giving advice	5	4	3	2	1
19.	Provide concrete feedback to others they can use	5	4	3	2	1
20.	Am comfortable with silence	5	4	3	2	1

Paraphrasing

Paraphrasing is restating what has been said, without parroting, in order to give the speaker your understanding of what he or she said. This way, the speaker has an opportunity to clear up any misunderstanding. Paraphrasing refers to content and is a part of reflecting, which includes both content and feelings.

Paraphrasing reduces confusion and misunderstandings that can easily occur. We tend to hear what is said through a perceptual screen influenced by our physical and emotional state as well as by our reaction to the speaker. In addition, there are times when speakers do not say what they intend to say. Paraphrasing allows for early corrections.

Learning to restate what you hear may be difficult and uncomfortable at first. Thinking of what words to use so that the speaker does not hear his or her exact words quoted back takes some practice. Judging when paraphrasing is needed is another skill that must be developed. In order to be effective, paraphrasing must be practiced.

You should use paraphrasing when a speaker is being overly general and you want more specificity. For example, if the speaker says that he or she would make a good counselor, you might paraphrase to see if your perception of a good counselor is the same as his or hers. In this case, you might say something like, "You see yourself as being able to guide others to help themselves?"

Another time paraphrasing is helpful is when the speaker's comments suggest examples of the topic to you. For example, if the speaker says "We are not getting qualified students in the program" you can paraphrase by saying, "Do you mean that too many students are failing, or that the quality of work in your class has decreased, or that test scores are lower than those of a few years ago?

Situations when paraphrasing is useful include when complex or complicated directions are given, when the speaker has used vague or general terms, when an example provides clarification, and when either the speaker or the receiver has strong emotional involvement. It is not necessary to paraphrase every statement. However, it is a component in active listening.

Reflecting

Reflection involves both the content and feelings involved in the message. It has the same purposes as paraphrasing: to reduce misunderstandings, promote clarity, and convey understanding of meaning to the speaker. The most important thing to remember is that the perceived feelings should be clearly identified and labeled.

Effective reflection involves attending, an openness to experiencing, and an ability to describe or label feelings. Learning a feeling language is an important part of developing reflecting skills. To get started, you can work on expanding your vocabulary with particular attention to words describing mild forms of intense emotions. For example, if a speaker is annoyed and you term the emotion as anger, he or she will probably reject the label and feel that you have misunderstood him or her.

Here are some guidelines for reflecting:

- Identify the underlying message (usually an emotion) and name the emotion you hear.

- Be tentative and paraphrase to check for accuracy.

- Be alert to connections or links to other verbalizations.

Ineffective Communication

There are some communication behaviors the leader should avoid, including speaking for others or the whole instead of making personal statements, asking inappropriate questions, using clichés, and exhibiting defensiveness. These kinds of communication promote inaccuracy of perceptions, game-playing behavior, hiding of the real self (a kind of deception), and feelings of being manipulated.

Following are some ineffective communication styles that tend to arouse hostile feelings and promote resistance. Some of these styles have positive points, as they can be used for appropriate circumstances. For example, in the military there are times when an authoritative response is called for. However, a psychoeducational group leader has little or no need for any of the styles described below.

The authoritarian is ineffective because he or she assumes a status differential. The authoritarian gives orders, and expects those orders to be followed. He or she becomes impatient if there appears to be any questioning of the "orders," and this attitude tends to dampen interaction between other group members.

The criticizer points the finger of blame, criticizes, and moralizes. This style of communication uses "oughts" and "shoulds" and tends to arouse guilt feelings in others. The criticizer does not seem pleased with anything or anybody, and tends to alienate others by making them feel inadequate no matter what they do.

The expert knows *all* the answers, and is not shy about imposing them on others. He or she does not wait to be asked for an opinion, but rushes in and overwhelms others with his or her "expertise." Experts tend to think they know a lot about everything.

The analyst always wants to tell others about their motives and underlying reasons for their feelings and behaviors. These people are even more dangerous when they know a little about human growth and behavior, especially if they know personality theory. Other group members tend to avoid the analyst because his or her communication style arouses hostile, angry feelings. Analyzing can be of use in a therapy session, but is not useful and may be dangerous outside of the therapeutic relationship.

The optimist, while seemingly benign, is a problem communicator. We all like to interact with upbeat, optimistic people. They make us feel good and promote hopefulness. However, the eternal optimist is off-putting, because he or she uses this optimism to avoid seeing or dealing with real problems and seeks to minimize or ignore his or her own and others' feelings.

The protector is a problematic type to deal with in a group. People who have difficulty dealing with anxiety-provoking situations and those who are emotionally expressive naturally tend to rush in to soothe, rescue, or protect in some way. The message they send to others is that the others need their help. The truth is that protectors are unable or unwilling to deal with their own feelings of discomfort and seek to minimize others' feelings in an effort to minimize their own. This style is difficult to deal with because, when their help is rejected, protectors feel hurt and others feel guilty, making for a real catch-22 situation.

The interrogator puts others in the "hot seat" because his or her questioning and probing, ostensibly used to get at the facts, makes others uncomfortable. Questions have their role, and this is addressed in the section on "Questioning" later in this chapter.

The magician is a lot like the eternal optimist. He or she tries to make problems, issues, and concerns disappear by refusing to acknowledge their existence. Whereas the eternal optimist brushes aside concerns by minimizing their impact, the magician tries to make them disappear completely by not thinking or talking about them. When the problem resurfaces, the magician shifts the topic to something less threatening. Others feel put down or discounted when the magician communicates with them.

The generalizer uses words like "always" and "never" frequently. Generalizers tend to categorize and make judgments about "all" instead of seeing others as individuals or situations as varied. The terms "always" and "never" rarely are appropriate when talking about people's behavior.

The accuser arouses hostility in others by calling names, labeling, and putting other on the defensive. Communication is ineffective or ceases completely when people feel attacked or labeled in some way. This kind of accusing communication is designed to put others at a disadvantage and to put the accuser at an advantage.

Speaking for Others.   When you do not use personal statements, but instead use terms like "we," "the group," or "all of us," you are modeling and encouraging the use of indirect and ineffective communication. It is much more effective for the leader and members to take responsibility for their own communications by making personal statements. There are times when you will point out what the group is doing; this is not speaking for the group.

Questioning

Questioning can be used effectively *if certain points are used to make a conscious choice* to question or not to question. All too often, questions are used inappropriately, leading to ineffective communications. There are three major uses for questions:

1. to obtain data and information,

2. to clarify and avoid misunderstandings, and

3. to pinpoint something in order to take immediate action.

Statements usually are more appropriate in other situations.

The primary rule of thumb for a question is to obtain *needed* data. I emphasize the word *needed* because, in most counseling situations, additional data is *not* needed. For example, a group member may be talking about an argument with a boss. Often, another group member or the leader will ask, "Has this happened before?" or "What kind of person is he?" or "Who else was there?"

This information is not needed. What you are dealing with is the speaker's experience and his or her feelings. When I point this out to students in my group counseling classes, the response is generally, "I was trying to understand." We then explore that objective further to determine how the questioned information aids in understanding. Most of the time, it does not give any further information useful for understanding. Questioning such as this serves to keep the focus off the speaker and his or her reactions.

There are times when questions are useful for clarification, of course: Verbalizations may be vague, rambling, ambiguous, or confusing. In these cases, questions can help us focus on the essentials and promote understanding of the message and the intent of the speaker. By asking the speaker if our identification of the point is correct, we help to clarify his or her communication. The group leader needs to develop this skill and use it effectively.

Pinpointing is needed in situations where prompt and precise action needs to be taken. These usually are crises, such as in an accident in which someone has been hurt. Group leaders may never face this purpose for questions.

Types of Questions.   Benjamin (1987) proposed five types of questions: direct, indirect, open, closed, and double.

> **Direct questions** are the ones most easily identified. They are specific and to the point. The group leader uses the direct questions most often: for example, "How did you respond?" or "What did you do?" or "Is the agenda meeting your needs?"

> **Indirect questions** usually can be reframed into statements. Making a question into a statement may involve something as simple as changing the inflection at the end. For example, "You are leaving?" becomes "You are leaving." In the group you could say, "There seems to be a lot of tension" instead of "Is there tension in the group?" Indirect questions are usually somewhat rhetorical. The speaker either knows the answer or has an opinion. But instead of saying so directly, he or she puts it in the form of a question, in part, so that personal ownership of the answer or opinion does not have to be assumed.

Open questions allow the responder the freedom to decide what information to share. These questions may produce unintended results, be
confusing or threatening to the receiver, and open the door to
storytelling. Open questions are genuinely seeking information, and
the speaker has no preconceived ideas about what information he or
she wants, but is willing to use what is presented.

Closed questions seek to limit the response to specific information or
answers. When specific information is needed, a direct, closed question is appropriate. One difficulty with closed questions is that they
may limit the answers given *too much*. In fact, the answer may not
give the questioner the information he or she needs because it is too
limited. For example, asking someone if he or she has finished an
activity allows only a yes-or-no answer. It does not take into consideration that they may never have engaged in the activity at all (for
example, the classic "Have you stopped beating your wife?"). Closed
questions may have the unintended effect of making the receivers
feel you are trying to trick them, or that you are not interested in their
answer if it has the potential for clashing with your opinion or pre-
conceptions.

Double questions put people in a bind by limiting the choice of answers
to one out of two when there may be others available. For example,
asking someone if they want to eat at X or at Y restaurant limits their
choices. There may be dozens of other eating places available, and
one of these could be more to their liking. Limiting choices can be
useful if these are, in fact, the only choices (for example, asking a
child if he or she wants to wear the green shirt or the yellow one when
those are the only two that coordinate with the rest of the outfit).

Developing Questioning Skills

Begin by becoming aware of how often you ask questions. One helpful
exercise is to tally the number of questions you ask in a day. Another has you go
an entire weekend without asking questions except as facts are needed.

The next step is be to become aware of the type of question you ask most
frequently and to determine how many of your questions are genuine requests
for information. For example, when you ask someone "How are you?" do you
really want to know, or is it just your way of being polite? How can the person
know if you are really interested or just being polite?

Begin to make a conscious evaluation of the need for asking a question. Can you make a statement instead? What advantage is there in asking a question?

Along with the growth in self-awareness, observe the your own behavior and that of others when asking questions. It is not unusual to ask many questions of the same person. In a sense, you bombard the person with questions. This can produce feelings of being attacked, and the resulting behavior is a defense, an attack, or a retreat. None of these behaviors promotes effective communication.

Stimulating Questions from Members. There is an art to encouraging members to actively participate, and stimulation of good questions is a good leadership skill. Good questions are those that show interest and relevancy, encourage participation and interaction, and point out the need for elaboration or clarification. The leader, however, cannot count on getting good questions from members, so an additional skill you need to develop is turning inadequate questions into good questions.

Reactions to Questions. Your first task as group leader is to examine your reactions to questions. Some common reactions are to become defensive, see questions as threats to your expertise or leadership, rush in to answer quickly, answer indirectly or with a question, and ignore the question. Responding appropriately to questions involves self-awareness, observation of the questioner, judging the appropriateness of a response, as well as other communication skills. Table 3.3 presents some suggestions for modifying reactions to questions. The subsequent discussion focuses on when it may be appropriate to use some of these reactions.

There are few rules or guidelines that are appropriate for all situations. The same is true for how to field questions from members. Becoming defensive or perceiving questions as threats speak to characteristics more than skills. These reactions are unique to the individual and usually have their antecedents in past personal experiences. Some of the other reactions may be appropriate under unique or differing circumstances.

Answering quickly may be useful for blocking undesired or inappropriate behavior. It may relieve tension and provide members with a sense of security.

Indirect answers also can be useful if, for example, some members lack the verbal facility or the confidence to ask direct questions. What they ask is not what they want to know, and the leader is aware of this. An indirect answer

TABLE 3.3
Reactions and Modifications to Receiving Questions

Reaction	Modification
Become defensive	Do not take questions personally. do not explain or apologize unless called for.
Questions perceived as threats	Suppress your anger. Identify why or what about the question is threatening. Do not express the anger, cut the person off, or discount them in some way.
Answering quickly	Mentally count 5 seconds. This gives you time to make sure you understand the question. Use clarification before answering.
Answering indirectly	Increasing consciousness of answering indirectly and make a conscious effort to give direct answers. Indirect answers leave people confused and frustrated.
Answering with a question	If you are not sure you understand, this may be appropriate. If, however, you do this under other circumstances, ask yourself what are you seeking to do. Some motives are; to make the other feel inept to show- off, to change the topic, etc. Reduce this behavior.
Ignoring the question	This is very similar to answering indirectly, but does not show as much respect. You may not wish to answer the question and should directly say so.

addresses the "real" question, and thus it can be more rewarding to the questioner than a direct answer.

Ignoring a question is tricky. You run the risk of alienating the speaker by making no response to a question. But there are a few circumstances where it may be more helpful to act as if the question had not been asked: for example, when the question is rhetorical, when it is asked and answered almost at once, and when basically the same question is asked by several members at the same time. Rather than ignoring questions, you could refocus, reframe, or explore implications.

Encouraging Questions. Once you have worked through your awareness of questioning behavior and reactions, it becomes easier to field questions from members. A larger concern then becomes how to encourage and stimulate questions. Some suggestions are presented below.

Determine your expectations. How do you want questions to be asked? Only when you give space for and request them? At any time? How do you want participants to ask questions—by raising their hands and being recognized or by jumping in? This is your group and you call these shots.

Inform group members of your expectations. Don't expect members to read your mind and know your expectations for them. If you are giving a mini-lecture during which questions will be a distraction, ask that questions be held until the end. If you do not mind being interrupted, say so.

Ask if members have any questions and pause a few seconds before continuing. There are some points at which a leader should open the floor to questions: for example, after reviewing the objectives and schedule, after giving directions for an exercise or activity, after disseminating information (e.g., a mini-lecture), and after a discussion.

Don't ask for questions just before a break. Questions and answers have a way of generating discussions. Sticking to the agreed-upon schedule is important, and these discussions can easily run over the time period. If one or two members have burning questions, you can remain a few minutes after group to answer them.

Inappropriate Questions

Inappropriate questions fall into several categories: limiting, putting someone on the spot, hypothetical, demands, reflected, rhetorical, and trapping. These are all ineffective ways of communicating. Questions should be limited to asking for needed information, not to communicate a position or point.

Limiting Questions. Limiting questions seek to contain or narrow the range of responses that can be given. The questioner is trying to obtain a particular response and asks questions in such a way that the desired answer is the most likely or the only one that can be given. Examples of limiting questions are these: "Don't you think that ... ?" or "Wouldn't you rather ... ?"

Hot Seat Questions.   It is relatively easy to put someone on the spot with questions. The purpose is to punish the speaker rather than to obtain needed information. Leading the speaker with questions is a form of manipulating him or her. Some individuals think that if they ask a series of questions, the other person will come to a desired conclusions. It is a kind of herding or locking in, to get one's own point across in an indirect way. It is much more effective to simply state your opinion or position, however, rather than asking unnecessary questions designed to put someone on the spot.

Hypothetical Questions.   Hypothetical questions are seldom used to elicit new information. If used to present a possible scenario in order to see how the other person would respond, a hypothetical question is useful and legitimate. Most often, however, the hypothetical question is used to probe for an answer to a question the speaker is afraid to ask directly.

Demands as Questions.   Questions such as "When are you going to ... ?" are implied demands. The questioner is not really interested in gaining new information, the question is a goad or a command to do something.

Questions to Hide One's Wants or Needs.   Some people are reluctant to state what they want. They disguise this with questions about what the other person's wants or preferences are. There are times when both parties wind up doing something neither wants because of indirect communication through questions.

Rhetorical Questions.   Rhetorical questions usually are followed by a phrase that assumes approval in advance (e.g., "Right?" "Okay?"). Such statements or requests also may be preceded with "Don't you think that ... ?" or "Isn't it true that ... ?" Rhetorical questions are framed in such a way that the desired response is assured, not to elicit new information or opinions.

Some people have developed the habit of asking questions instead of making statements. Group leaders need to become aware of their communication behavior and take steps to limit questions to requests for information.

Chapter 4

LEADERSHIP, LEARNING LEVELS, AND INVOLUNTARY MEMBERS

DISTRIBUTED LEADERSHIP

Groups go through stages and participants in a particular group may be at all levels, which calls for differing leadership strategies for both levels and stages.

Fiedler (1978) proposed a distributed function for group leaders based on the group needs. He proposed two functions: task and maintenance.

Task-oriented leaders take responsibility for the direction and functioning of the group. They make decisions, and group members are willing to follow. Tasks are clear, unambiguous, and can be structured.

Maintenance-oriented leaders concentrate on having members participate in shared responsibility and decision making. These leaders are most effective when the task is somewhat clear (although there may be some ambiguity) and members are willing and able to assume some responsibility for the functioning of the group.

Both functions can be used effectively in psychoeducational groups. Task functions are most important in pregroup preparation and in the beginning stages. As members become more comfortable and trusting of themselves, of the group, and of the leader, they assume more responsibility for the functioning of the group and the leader assumes a maintenance function. It may take time and experience to know when to shift functions, but both are useful and both can be detrimental if used inappropriately.

SITUATIONAL LEADERSHIP

Hershey and Blanchard (1977) proposed a theory of situational leadership that classified leadership behaviors along two dimensions: task and relationship. They used the two dimensions in conjunction with the maturity level of group members. *Task behaviors* are telling, explaining, and clarifying, and are primarily one-way (i.e., leader to members). *Relationship behaviors* are those the leader uses to give emotional support and to facilitate group progress and are characterized by two-way communication.

Hershey and Blanchard (1977) defined maturity in terms of a person's extent of achievement motivation, degree of willingness to assume responsibility, past experiences, and educational levels. The degree of maturity exhibited also is related to the newness or novelty of the task. For example, a highly educated adult may have little or no knowledge of a given task, and so would exhibit low maturity.

These categories produce four interactions of task and relationship, with four related leadership behaviors: high task-high relationship uses "telling" behaviors; high task-low relationship uses "selling" behaviors; low task-low relationship uses "participating" behaviors; low task-high relationship uses "delegating" behaviors.

Both of these leadership theories take into account the variations in needs and abilities of group members, the tasks, and the group itself. However, neither describes how to recognize learning levels in the group and what the leader can do to facilitate group development.

LEARNING LEVELS AND LEADERSHIP STRATEGIES

Leaders of psychoeducational groups need to use a combination of learning theory and group development. Theories of learning, including principles of instruction, provide a framework for presenting material for the intended

TABLE 4.1
Levels for Participants and Leadership Strategies

Participants' Level	Characterization	Leadership Strategy
Low		
Little understanding, unclear goals, ambiguous	Confusion, resistance, questioning, seeks clarification	Directing Structuring
Low to Moderate		
Lacks clarity of task, personal involvement, "wait and see" attitude	Insecure, less confusion, less resistance	Motivating Encouraging
Moderate		
Understanding of task, self-motivation and personal involvement	Responsible, participating, initiating	Involving Mutuality
High		
Understanding and appreciation of tasks, very motivated, eager to proceed	Works independently and as a member of the team	Empowering Delegating

audience so that they can understand it, apply it and retain it. Theory presents a basis for learning and suggests strategies.

Knowledge of group development allows you to make optimal use of techniques and strategies. Group development stages suggest when and how to present material so that it can be effectively received and used.

Table 4.1 presents an overview of the leadership and learning levels most often encountered in psychoeducational groups. These levels were developed using theories of learning and stages of group development. They are not dependent on members' intelligence or amount of education, although these factors may come into play for the advanced levels. The table presents simplified ways of identifying levels, associating them with behaviors, and suggesting leadership strategies. I strongly encourage you to learn more about typical behaviors expected at different ages and behaviors expected in different stages of a group.

Table 4.1 is more useful if these points are kept in mind:

- Age plays a role but is not critical in determining participants' level of learning.

- Members may move through all levels in one group session, or may only move through one or two levels.

- The leadership strategy used must be consistent with the leader's personality, but all leaders need to use some form of each leadership strategy.

Low Level

When participants are behaving at a "low" level, you must do more directing and structuring. Decisions about what to do and how to do it are beyond members' capabilities at this point. All participants are dealing with issues of safety, trust, inclusion, and competence, regardless of their educational or experience level. Explaining, clarifying, and reflecting are useful for reducing ambiguity and answering unasked or indirect questions about the "real" issues. Some members may be so fearful they never move beyond this level. They cannot, and you should neither push them nor expect more than they can do.

Low to Moderate Level

When participants reach a low to moderate learning level, some of their "real" issues have been sufficiently addressed so that they evidence less resistance. Members appear willing to give you and the process a chance to meet their needs. Participation still is tentative, there is an air of wariness, but many members mask these feelings and wear a facade of cooperativeness and involvement. You can increase participation and involvement by encouraging and motivating.

Again, your major focus is not on the task, but on the indirect and unspoken feelings of participants. Nonverbal behaviors are useful here. Eye contact with head nods, a slight forward lean, warmth, and showing interest and respect can contribute to participants' feelings of encouragement and motivation. You should plan activities that can be easily understood and accomplished with little or no frustration. You will be very active and busy with participants at this level as responses need to be immediate and directed to the individuals.

Moderate Level

Few participants begin a group at the moderate level. If you have any in a group, you will find them to be of immense help. Their modeling of desired attitudes and behaviors, confidence in the process and the leader, and willingness to participate promote feelings of trust and safety for other members.

However, most groups will not start off with participants at this level. The good news is that the group can get to this level in a short time if you facilitate the process. Building confidence in the group process and leader, and attending to safety and trust issues encourage development to this level. Once this level is attained, you can become less active as members will interact with each other more and communications will not be primarily to and through you.

A leader must have confidence and trust in the group process and in the group members in order for this level to be satisfactory. You must relinquish some power and control and let members assume some responsibility for the functioning of the group. This means a switch in strategy and roles, becoming less directive and structuring and more mutually participatory.

High Level

When participants reach the high level, they can effectively function independently as team members. Attaining this level is accomplished over time with considerable interaction of members. Members have to know each other well and feel accepted, cared for, and respected. You can facilitate this process, but it cannot be hurried. Each and every member must attain the level, and some members take longer to arrive than others. You must take care not to become discouraged at a slow pace; it does take time.

INVOLUNTARY MEMBERS AND LEADER TASKS

A major factor in deciding on appropriate leadership strategies is if members are voluntary or involuntary participants. This can have a significant impact on participant level, expected behavior, and group development.

There are many instances in which members of a group are involuntary participants. Members may attend because they were ordered to do so by an authority (such as a court or school principal), as a condition for continued participation in a job or school, as part of a program for contained or incarcerated people (such as inpatients, felons, or juvenile group home residents), or as part of their educational training (such as groups for mental health professionals). The reasons for involuntary attendance may vary, but many of the same characteristics are shared and must be taken into account by the group leader.

Some involuntary participants will view group as an opportunity to learn, grow, and develop more effective ways of relating. Others will be defiant, resistant, or resentful about having to participate. Some will be openly hostile and others passive-aggressive. You can expect that involuntary participation will result in more barriers than voluntary participation.

It is useful to acknowledge the involuntary nature of their participation early on and give members an opportunity to express their feelings about it. This can be done during the screening interview or during the first session. You may also need to be more specific about what will be done in group and what is expected of group members. These members may be more fearful, as they usually can expect unpleasant consequences for failure.

Constraints to Active Participation

Resistance and defenses are more intense for involuntary participants because they lack power and control: They do not freely choose to be in the group. Another reason for resistance is a fear of the unknown. All group members share some of this fear, but it may be more intense for involuntary participants because they have been thrust into an ambiguous situation not of their choosing, and they often do not know what to expect or what is expected of them.

Fear of harm plays an important role for involuntary participants as well. They may fear that disclosed information will be given to others and used against them, or that other group members will use it to further their own personal ends. They may fear they will be evaluated and found inadequate.

Resentment at being forced to participate may also be a part of resistance. Such resentment may be focused on the authority ordering attendance, but it is more likely to be generalized and widespread. Everyone but them is at fault for their having to be in the group. Resentment may be more openly expressed and demonstrated by some members, such as court-ordered participants, than by others; but it is present, in some degree, in all involuntary participants. Some simply mask the resentment better than others.

The Leader's Role

As the leader of a group with involuntary participants, you must be prepared to deal with their fears, resistance, defenses, and resentments. Knowing that these are not only likely *but are certain to be manifested in some way* allows you to better plan to address them. Your primary tasks are to adequately address safety and trust issues, to diffuse hostility and resentment, to empower members to decide their own level of participation and disclosure, to have clear goals and objectives, to understand boundary issues and respect them, and to refrain from power struggles.

Address Safety and Trust Issues. The first task of the group leader is to directly respond to unspoken or indirectly communicated safety and trust issues. You should provide specific guidelines for expected participation. If confidentiality can be maintained, you should say so. If, on the other hand, agency guidelines or legal constraints prevent you from maintaining confidentiality, you must notify the participants of this at the beginning.

Diffuse Hostility and Resentment. You can take steps to diffuse hostility, resentment, or defensiveness that may be directly or indirectly expressed. This, of course, is much easier to do in a small group, as you can make eye contact with each member and use some nonverbal behaviors to promote trust. One way to diffuse these feelings is to acknowledge that you know and appreciate these feelings about being forced to attend. If the group size is manageable, have session around in which each member responds to this question: "What do you like or dislike most about having to attend this group?" Or, "What would make this group experience worthwhile for you?"

Let Members Decide Their Levels of Participation. Empower members to take charge of their group experience by giving them permission to decide how much they can or will participate. Assure them you will not push or demand responses, but you will provide opportunities and give encouragement. Giving them some measure of control, and following through on it, helps promote feelings of safety and trust.

Set Goals and Objectives. Another beginning step is to have clear goals and objectives and to review them with members. Develop attainable goals and be willing to modify them if necessary. Ask if there are any goals or objectives the members wish included, or if there are any about which they have reservations. If you can be open and flexible, members can buy into the goals and objectives. which will lead to more personal involvement in achieving the task and in the group.

Respect Boundary Issues. It is very helpful to delineate firm and permeable boundaries for involuntary participants. Take some time to discuss boundary issues such as the following:

- What topics members and the leader can discuss with people not in the group, and under what conditions.

- What material should not be discussed with people not in the group.

- What group content can be talked about between members in the group when they are outside the group (e.g., socializing).

- What data the leader has to share with other professionals, and in what form (i.e., with or without personal identifying data).

- What use will be made of the information shared by the members.

Talking over these issues helps members to better judge what is appropriate participation for them.

One boundary that is under the leader's control is time. Adhering to the specified schedule provides support for consistency. Many involuntary participants have not had clear and unambiguous boundaries before. Ambiguity promotes feelings of insecurity and wariness. You cannot be expected to address and allay all of their insecurities, but you can provide firm time boundaries so that at least one thing is consistent.

Refrain from Power Struggles. A final suggestion is this: *Do not engage in power struggles with members.* Many members will attempt to engage you in power struggles, either to test you or because it is their characteristic way of behaving or relating. Remember this: "When power is unequally distributed, the low-power person will automatically distrust the high-power person because she (he) knows that those with power have a tendency to use it for their own interests" Walton (1987). As the group leader, you are seen as the high-power person, and members may fear your use of such power because of past experiences.

You are not engaging in a power struggle when you develop guidelines for expected behaviors, do not permit physical or verbal violence, or protect a member from emotional abuse or a barrage of questions. These are legitimate leader behaviors designed to protect group members and provide for effective group functioning.

Ethical Guidelines for Involuntary Participants

These ethical issues are the most important when you are dealing with involuntary participants.

Freedom of Exit.   With the exception of students and professionals, most involuntary participants do not feel they have the freedom to exit. While it may be possible to physically exit or to refuse to participate, the alternatives (e.g., jail) are often worse. This promotes feelings of being trapped and of being forced to do things against their will. For many involuntary participants, this increases defiance and passive aggressiveness, while others are more open in their hostility.

As group leader, you will receive the brunt of participants' feelings about lack of freedom to exit. Many participants are not able to accept personal responsibility, cannot or will not express their negative feelings to the official(s) who sent them to group, and are fearful of what will happen if they stay or if they leave.

Confidentiality.   Typically, there are more limits on what can be kept confidential with involuntary clients. Legal, moral, and training issues often prevent confidentiality from being complete. For example, case notes sometimes must be kept and can be read by others; consultation with supervisors may be mandated or encouraged, certain crimes (e.g., incest) must be reported to the proper officials; and participants who might harm themselves or others must be screened. Further, in a closed setting—such as a group home, hospital, or jail—there is no way to fully ensure that the content of sessions can be kept confidential.

Group members must be informed at the beginning of group what cannot be kept confidential. Ideally, the issue of confidentiality and constraints should be discussed in screening or pregroup sessions as well as in the first session. However, if it is not possible to do so prior to the first session, you must initiate the discussion early in the first group.

Screening.   Screening of potential group members is desirable. Even if you are not able to reject members because of policies or rules, it is still desirable to have an individual pregroup interview session. It may also be possible to reject those who would be disruptive to the group if officials making decisions about participants can be shown sufficient reasons to do so. The screening interview could provide you with the rationale for your judgment.

Orienting and Providing Information

If you cannot schedule pregroup orienting sessions, you can use the first session for this purpose. Group work is scary for many participants; and when involuntary participation with possible negative consequences is added to the usual fears about participation, the situation is greatly exacerbated. An important thing to remember is that group business—goals, process, and so on—gets accomplished during orienting sessions also. Your time is not wasted in helping members understand what is expected of them, how they should behave, and what will be done in the group. Group participation is enhanced if you do adequate orientation.

Coercion and Pressure.   Although there is an element of coercion implicit for involuntary participants, you must take care to ensure that neither identification with the aggressor nor displacement of feelings around the coercion has a negative impact on the group. It is not possible to prevent either of these from happening, but if you realize that they are possible and take steps to neutralize their impact, you can help both individual members and the functioning of the group.

Identification with the aggressor produces behavior similar to that perceived held by the "authorities." Examples of such behavior are giving orders and expecting to be obeyed, expecting deference from others and becoming angry or enraged if it is not given, sadistic acts that are passive, and so on. While these behaviors may be characteristic for some members, others may assume them as a defense mechanism.

Displacement is a common defense mechanism used by many people for various situations. Under these circumstances it may be manifested in the group and become a barrier to progress. This is one reason it is so important to get the issue of coercion on the table early and the feelings around it expressed. You usually can expect to be the target of displaced feelings, but other members may also be targets.

Dual Relationships.   It is difficult to avoid dual relationships with involuntary group participants. Even if you have only "arms length" input into any evaluation or decision, you cannot avoid it altogether; you probably will be perceived by group members as having an evaluative role and function. For example, in training groups for professionals the leader may also be the clinical supervisor. It may not be possible to separate out the impact of group participation and disclosure on the perceptions of clinical behavior/expertise. The group leader/supervisor typically makes every effort to do so, but as these effects and interactions are not clearly understood, one cannot be sure that the roles and functions are kept separate.

There is also the issue of power differential. When the group leader also has an evaluative function, no matter how slight, there is an increase in the power differential between leader and members. Members may perceive the power differential as being greater than it actually is, and relate to the leader in terms of their perception. This perception can increase mistrust, inhibit disclosure, intensify resistance and defenses, promote deference, or prevent honest participation.

Another issue is that of the leader's objectivity. Having more than one role and function has an impact on the leader. His or her objectivity can be impaired because of interactions, behaviors, and relationships resulting from group participation. Countertransference, projection, and projective identification are all possible for the leader and can lead to impaired objectivity. The leader's objectivity is subject to manipulation by group members and can carry over into other leader roles and functions.

PROBLEM BEHAVIORS AND THEIR GOALS

Most problem behaviors in psychoeducational groups can be categorized as overparticipation, underparticipation, or socializing.

Overparticipating members monopolize, tell stories, interrupt when others are speaking, and use other distracting behaviors.

Underparticipating members withdraw, are silent, make few responses even when directly addressed, and may do the minimum required for an activity.

The socializer engages in side conversations when others are talking, interacts repeatedly with the same person(s), introduces topics at variance with what is being discussed under the guise of being friendly, starts conversations instead of participating in the activity, is late coming back from breaks, and so on. The socializer does not act alone, you are likely to have two or more in the group.

The following sections describe these behaviors in more detail and give suggestions for dealing with them.

Overparticipation

The overparticipating member wants attention from the leader and from other members. At first, you may appreciate the input. Having a group member respond or initiate questions can energize the group, which helps the process move along. It does not take long, however, for one member's overinvolvement to become a real problem. The dilemma for the leader is how to block overparticipating behavior without squelching the member or discounting him or her in some way.

Remember that other members will assume that how you treat this person is how you will treat them, *whether or not they engage in the same type of behavior*. Sometimes, the group will handle the behavior by confronting the member with its impact on them. For example, if one member interrupts others frequently, at some point another member may ask the interrupter if he or she would let the speaker finish.

Storytelling and Monopolizing. The task of blocking monopolizing and storytelling behavior can be a difficult one. Most often, the group has not progressed to the point where members feel safe handling the leader's intervention. One rule of thumb is to let the storytelling or monopolizing behavior occur the first time without comment. Try to link what the person is talking about to the goals of the group. Express appreciation for the member's input to encourage others to participate. After that, try to intervene before the storyteller gets started.

If several members want to speak, let others talk before the monopolizer. Call on reticent members by asking if they have comments. Do not ignore the storyteller, just try to limit the time he or she has the floor. If necessary, you can break into a story with, "I am sorry to interrupt you, but it is time for a break (or the next scheduled activity, or to move on if we are to stay on schedule). I would like to get back to you on that."

Physically Distracting Behaviors. Children and adolescents are more apt than adults to engage in physically distracting behaviors, such as pushing, getting out of their seats, and walking around. You should clearly articulate guidelines for expected group behaviors. These may be somewhat flexible, but are developed to ensure smooth running of the group and focus on the task. Member who engage in distracting behaviors can be gently and tentatively confronted. You might say, for example, "I am interested in what Joe is saying, but I find it hard to pay attention when you are making noise kicking the chair."

If the group has developed to a point where members can handle being reminded of the rules without feeling criticized or put down, a simple reminder of agreed upon behavior may be adequate.

Attention Seeking. Basically, you must decide to either ignore or attend to attention-getting behavior. Sometimes, ignoring the behavior causes it to stop because it is not reinforced. Sometimes the behavior will cease or be modified if some attention is received, because the goal is attained. At other times, attention simply escalates the behavior. You must judge the appropriate response.

Under- or Nonparticipation

The goals for under- or nonparticipation typically are rebellion, self-protection, or revenge.

Rebellion ("You cannot make me participate") usually occurs with involuntary group participants. They did not choose to be in group and, because they were forced or coerced in some way to attend, they will refuse to participate. The refusal may not be open and direct, but their lack of participation speaks volumes. The leader needs to go slow and not try to force participation, acknowledging that they, indeed, cannot be forced to participate.

For some, such as court-ordered participants, you may want to address the issue of involuntary participation openly and make the topic a part of the group process. Asking participants for their thoughts and feelings about the proposed group and its activities, and acknowledging that you can only encourage participation and cannot force it will allow some members to express their resistances. Generally, many will then cooperate, if only on a superficial level. You must model genuineness by not insisting that the under- or nonparticipant become more involved. Offer opportunities to become involved in the group, but do not push.

When under- or nonparticipation has the goal of *protecting the self*, you are wise to *let the member alone*. Even in a counseling/therapy group the member would be allowed to determine the level and extent of his or her participation. Safety and trust are critical issues for this member, and it is unlikely that these issues can be sufficiently addressed in a psychoeducational group because of the limited time frame. You can encourage input by asking these members directly, from time to time, if they have any comments. Acknowledge any comments with a response to reinforce the positive behavior of participation. Ask nonthreatening questions that do not require self-disclosure or opinions.

The *revenge* goal is similar to the rebellion goal, but it has the added component of trying to hurt others. These members are "getting back" at those who hurt them by trying to hurt others. These members are the sullen, hostile, silent ones. There is a kind of threat about their silence, whereas the rebellious member is not necessarily sullen and hostile. The best strategy is to leave these members alone but block any attacking behavior. Extend an invitation to participate, but openly acknowledge that you cannot make them participate and that you will respect their decision. If they must be present—that is, they do not have the freedom to leave—you can try asking them what the group can do to make the experience more meaningful for them.

Socializing

The socializer is having a grand old time. He or she is talkative, enjoys interacting with others, may giggle or laugh a lot, and wants to be involved with others and have them involved with him or her. In counseling/therapy groups, other members often will confront the socializer. But in short-term groups, the group usually does not take responsibility. Further, the task function of psychoeducational groups makes it less likely that personal development is a significant goal, and the group likely will not confront the socializer.

Strategies you can use in dealing with socializers include physically moving toward them and standing near them, making sure they are in different groups, speaking to them during break about the behavior and its impact on the group, and directly soliciting their input by calling on them by name.

Chapter 5

ETHICAL ISSUES
AND HELPFUL FACTORS

Leaders of psychoeducational groups should follow the same ethical guide-lines as do leaders of counseling and therapy groups. Although not all of the guidelines are applicable to psychoeducational groups (e.g., screening), most have relevance for the leader of psychoeducational groups. I encourage you to study the Association for Specialists in Group Work (ASGW, 1990) guidelines and to incorporate them as part of your practice in group work.

MAJOR ETHICAL ISSUES

There are 16 categories for ethical guidelines in psychoeducational groups, which are listed below.

Orientation and providing information	Screening
Confidentiality	Voluntary/involuntary participation
Leaving a group	Coercion and pressure
Imposing counselor values	Equitable treatment
Dual relationships	Use of techniques
Goal development	Consultation

Termination from the group   Evaluation and follow-up

Referrals   Professional development

Each of these will be briefly described, and suggested applicability to psychoeducational groups will be explained in this section.

Orientation

Group members should be adequately prepared to participate fully in the group experience. You can reduce much of the confusion and ambiguity that exists for all beginning groups by providing as much information about the experience as possible prior to beginning the group. Groups members should know what to expect so they can make informed decisions about participation. A process and guidelines are presented in the section on "Pregroup Planning" in chapter 7.

Screening

Screening group members to determine their suitability for the proposed group has limited application for psychoeducational groups. Groups that emphasize development, social skills, life skills, or those that involve personal issues may benefit from screening members. However, groups for team building, time management, and other training functions probably will not derive much benefit from screening, nor will the leader be in a position to determine group membership. It is possible to screen via a written questionnaire, but if you do not have the authority to exclude members, the questionnaire serves no useful purpose.

Confidentiality

As an ethical issue, confidentiality has many of the same constraints as does screening. Psychoeducational groups usually do not deal with matters that demand confidentiality. Some groups do deal with personal issues, however, and the group leader should emphasize confidentiality. You can approach the issue by assuring members that discussion of content outside the group is acceptable, but identification of members and their issues is not. Confidentiality is more of a concern for group counseling/therapy than it is for psychoeducational groups.

Participation

Voluntary/involuntary participation is a complex issue. What constitutes voluntary participation? For example, students preparing for a degree in counseling are expected to participate in a growth group. Is this voluntary or involuntary? Because this is a complex ethical issue, it is addressed more fully in the section on "Ethical Guidelines for Involuntary Participants" in chapter 4.

Leaving the Group

As a group leader, you must sometimes provide the opportunity for a member to leave the group in a constructive way that takes into account the feelings of the member who is leaving and the feelings of the members who remain. It is assumed that members have the right to leave a group, although there may be consequences for doing so. This ethical issue may apply more to counseling/therapy groups, but it has implications for any group that meets over time. Leaders of psychoeducational should be prepared to cope with premature termination for a variety of reasons. While it may not be as much of an issue for these groups, leaving still has an impact on group members.

Coercion and Pressure

Leaders have the moral, legal, and ethical responsibility to protect members from "physical threats, intimidation, coercion, and undue peer pressure" (ASGW, 1991). While such acts may be more intense and dangerous in counseling/therapy groups, the potential for harm is present in psychoeducational groups. Presenting clear guidelines for expected behaviors for group members, blocking inappropriate behaviors, and assessing the effects of exercises and activities will help you meet this guideline.

Imposing Counselor Values

The greatest safeguard against imposing counselor values is the self-awareness of the group leader. Knowing your values, attitudes, and beliefs allows you to understand the potential impact they may have on others, especially if you have difficulty accepting differing ones. It is acceptable for a leader to appropriately disclose his or her values, attitudes, and beliefs; it is not acceptable for the leader to insist that group members follow them. Although psychoeducational groups are more task-focused, values play an important role in many aspects of the group. Therefore, it is important that you be aware of your personal values and take care not to impose them on the group.

Equitable Treatment

It is important to recognize and respect the differences of all group members. Differences such as gender, religion, race/ethnicity, lifestyle, age, and disability are important. The group leader should know enough about cultural and diversity issues to be sensitive to these differences and to ensure that members are not discriminated against because of them.

Dual Relationships

The issue of dual relationships is a troubling and complex one. Some dual relationships are easy to identify, for example, sexual, supervisory, and family. Others are not so easy to define, for example, student-teacher and social contact. The leader of a psychoeducational group may also be in a work relationship with one or more participants in the group. Does this constitute a dual relationship? There is no easy answer. It depends on whether there is the potential for the leader's objectivity and professional judgment to be negatively affected or for it to have a negative impact on a group member. Leaders of psychoeducational groups should give careful consideration to the issue of dual relationships and do everything in their power to ensure that these do not impact the group or members.

Use of Techniques

Group leaders should not use techniques for which they have not received training. It may be tempting to try new techniques, but doing so may imperil group members in ways that the leader did not anticipate. This ethical guideline is somewhat tempered for psychoeducational groups when you are using structured exercises that are new but similar to those for which you were trained. Techniques usually refer to a category (e.g., gestalt games, imagery), not to a variation. The primary concern is that group members not be put in situations that are dangerous for them.

Developing Goals

More learning and greater satisfaction occurs when goals for the group are consistent with individual members' goals. Leaders of psychoeducational groups generally set the goals, sometimes in collaboration with the organization for which the group is being conducted (e.g., team building); and there are occasions when goals are set in consultation with group members. Most often, however, it is up to the leader to set the goals.

This ethical issue appears to be more relevant when groups are small, personal issues are the focus, and there will be more than one session. However, leaders of all psychoeducational groups should be aware that the group is enhanced when members help set the goals, and that goals are more likely to be achieved if members have vested interests. Even when you must set the goals yourself, it may be useful to review them at the beginning of the group, telling members that the goals can be changed if members feel the goals are not meeting their needs or expectations. If you have adequately researched the subject and know relevant information about the participants, probably only a few changes will be recommended.

Consultation

The ethical issue of consultation applies when the leader is in training, there is more than one session, and personal issues are the focus of the group. Consultation refers to the leader receiving supervision, establishing rules for between-session meetings with members, limiting what the leader can discuss with others (e.g., case management), and when the leader has a dual role: responsibility to the members and responsibility to the agency (e.g., a probation office). However, members need to know in advance what content will be discussed or shared with others who are in authority or outside the group. That way, members can be more self-governing.

Terminating a Member

There are times when a member must be terminated from the group for his or her own good or for the good of the group. Disruptive members, those who have overwhelming personal or emotional disturbances that impede their participation, and violent or abusive members are some examples. Leaders of psychoeducational groups are unlikely to run into this situation often. If, for some reason, a member does have to be terminated, you must arrange for a constructive termination that takes into account the needs of the member being terminated and those of members who remain. You may need to bring in a consultant to aid in the process, especially if you are not experienced in this kind of termination issue.

Evaluation and Follow-Up

Provisions for evaluating the group should be made during the planning period. It is useful if the evaluation is in written form, although oral feedback also can be solicited. If the group is an open-ended one, you can use formative evaluation to help make adjustments to the process. There may also be opportunities to have follow-up evaluation. Usually, the return rate for evaluation forms in psychoeducational groups is poor. Once participants have returned home, other activities take priority and the evaluation does not get completed. You should complete some form of evaluation, but follow-up may not be possible or necessary.

Referrals

Referrals can help participants, and leaders should have some knowledge of community resources, especially those relating to topics being presented in the group. If you are unfamiliar with the community or resources available, you should refer members to an individual who does have that knowledge.

Professional Development

Professional development is expected for group leaders. While the leader may be an expert in the topic, there is always more information, new techniques, and more understanding of group dynamics to be learned. It is important for group leaders to continue to prepare themselves to conduct groups, and this can occur through classes, seminars, workshops, conferences, and home study. The primary responsibility for continued professional development lies with the leader.

HELPFUL GROUP FACTORS

There are certain factors that have been found to enhance group counseling/therapy. Yalom (1995) proposed 11 such factors and presented research findings to support their effectiveness. The 11 factors are listed below.

> **Universality:** knowing that others share similar issues, problems, concerns, or feelings

Instillation of hope: knowing that people in situations similar to yours do improve and, in some cases, problems can be resolved

Altruism: the unselfish giving to others with no expectation of return or gratitude; does not mean giving advice or opinions about what one should or ought to do

Imitative behavior: the modeling of more effective and appropriate ways of relating and communicating

Development of socializing techniques: learning how one is perceived by others and practicing new ways of relating and communicating

Imparting of information: learning new and unfamiliar material relating to oneself

Interpersonal learning: becoming more aware of personal issues through the feedback of others

Cohesiveness: when group members trust each other enough to engage in important and appropriate self-disclosure, care for each other, support and encourage each other

Catharsis: an emotional venting; expressing of deeply held, intense feelings that were pent up, repressed, or denied

Corrective recapitulation of the family of origin: group provides an opportunity for members to replay their roles in their families of origin and to experience different, and more desirable, responses and outcomes; members learn they are not trapped in these roles

Existential factors: basic existential factors of aloneness, death, responsibility, freedom, and will appear in group; acknowledging them openly helps members realize their universality, their never-ending nature, and can provide some understanding

Many of these factors also are present in psychoeducational groups and can be helpful, if not therapeutic. They manifest themselves in somewhat different ways than they do in counseling or therapy groups, and the group leader uses them in different ways. The purpose of the group also makes a difference in the appearance or absence of a factor and how it may be used. For example, a discussion group may lead into exploration of existential factors, but a team development group is unlikely to explore these issues. Further, exploration of personal issues with in-depth self-disclosure is not expected in psychoeducational groups, and the appearance of these factors usually will be on a more superficial level.

However, the leader of any psychoeducational group can make effective use of these factors. The first step is to accept that these factors enhance the process and progress of the group. The second step is to recognize their value and to begin to identify their appearance. The third step is to openly bring attention to the factor in appropriate ways, paying attention to timing. Finally, the fourth step is promoting or introducing the factor. Factors and steps will be discussed in the following sections. The factors are presented in categories ranging from "most likely to be present" to "least likely." What follows is an overall summary, and different groups may have a somewhat different ordering. It is important to remember that group members also may facilitate the emergence of a factor, it is not the sole responsibility of the leader.

THERAPEUTIC FACTORS MOST LIKELY TO APPEAR

Universality

This factor may be easy to identify in psychoeducational groups because members usually have several characteristics in common: They may be from the same organization, such as a school; have the same goal, such as anger management; be in the same age, racial/ethnic, or gender group; or have similar interests, as evidenced by their choice to attend the group, such as parenting classes.

Most people can easily identify the surface similarities, but a leader's expertise is evident when he or she can identify important subtle similarities and bring them to the group's attention. For example, it may appear that the only things a group of adolescents in an anger management group have in common are their age, their need to learn anger management, and their presence in the group. What the group leader may identify as similar to all or most members is a feeling of helplessness when they do not see how to gain or manage control of a situation; feelings that others seek to control them; and an inability to focus on and be aware of milder forms of anger. These universalities promote bonding and reduce feelings of isolation and alienation, such as feeling different.

It is the leader's responsibility to bring these commonalities to the attention of group members. Members seldom recognize deeper commonalities and tend to focus on differences, particularly on visible differences. The group bonds and becomes cohesive around similarities, but fragments and dissolves around differences. Developing the skill of linking will help you identify and introduce the factor of universality.

Altruism

Altruism often goes unrecognized, and often what is thought to be altruism is not, because the giver expects something in return. This factor can be helpful with members who are feeling helpless, hopeless, isolated, or useless. Children, in particular, benefit from knowing that they have something to give that is of value. They usually are on the receiving end, and few adults take the time and effort to help them understand that they have something to give that is valued by others.

Recognizing altruism is difficult because motives play a part, and this is an internal event that can only be inferred. The leader can model altruism, reinforce what appears to be altruism, and, in appropriate circumstances, describe altruism. An example of why altruism is difficult to identify can be illustrated in the following scenario. Group members are discussing a problem. One member tells the group that he or she addressed the problem in a particular way that is beneficial or gives suggestions for resolutions. Even an experienced leader will not always know if the suggestions are being offered to get attention, to garner admiration, to show the teller's superiority, to control or manipulate in some way, or out of altruism.

The leader can assume that there is not a hidden agenda until there is more evidence. If this is the only session, or there are very few sessions, the leader should acknowledge the contribution as being useful and make no determination about the giver's motives. One of the nice things about this factor is that if it is present it can be beneficial in indirect ways, and the leader can simply allow it to emerge.

Imitative Behavior

A major task for the group leader is to model appropriate behaviors. Many psychoeducational groups are designed to teach participants different ways of behaving, relating, or communicating. One way of learning is through observing and practicing. Modeling is a powerful technique for teaching new behaviors to those who may not have a clue how to behave, relate, or communicate differently than they do now. Telling someone how to do something is not as effective as showing him or her.

The leader also may recognize when group members are imitating other group members. Members do learn from each other as well as from the leader. It is helpful if the leader can recognize and reinforce desired behaviors through praise.

Imparting of Information

Giving factual information is one of the primary tasks for a psychoeducational group. Some of the group leader's responsibilities are teaching new and unfamiliar material and guiding the learner. However, the leader may not be the only one who has relevant information. Group members also know important pieces and should be encouraged to share and participate in imparting information. Be alert to advice-giving and "shoulds" and "oughts." These behaviors are not helpful and must be blocked or reframed into more helpful behaviors.

Imparting of information may be the easiest factor to recognize, since it is so obvious. The leader usually does not need to openly identify it. It is useful, however, to reinforce when members impart information by saying things like, "That is important to know. Thank you for bringing it to our attention." Other members then become encouraged to share information. The primary thing to remember is that you must limit the amount of information to what participants can absorb and use—not what you think they need or what you want to give. Too much information can be overwhelming, frustrating, and confusing.

FACTORS LIKELY TO APPEAR

Instillation of Hope

This factor is dependent on the type of group. It usually is associated with getting better, solving personal problems, and resolving personal issues. Many psychoeducational groups do not deal with these concerns; participants attend to learn more concrete and less personally related material.

However, there are some groups for which personal issues, problems, or concerns are the focus; in such groups, this factor would be in the "most likely to appear" category. In these instances, the leader must take steps to introduce "hope" into the group.

Hope is what allows individuals to continue to work on and through their concerns. We have to hope that the distress or pain will end someday. Further, hope is one rationale for participating in the group in the first place; why go through the experience if nothing will change?

Hope can be introduced by giving examples of how the group has helped others—personal experiences are particularly helpful—how group experiences are structured to address issues, and anticipated outcomes. Participants often ask, directly or indirectly, "How is this supposed to help me?" You can anticipate the question and provide the information before it is asked. By doing so, you increase participants' confidence that their problem will be adequately addressed the group. It is helpful if there are group members who have resolved or constructively dealt with the problem or something similar. Seeing others who have "come through it" gives hope to members that they, too, can achieve. Effective leaders capitalize on these success stories. They can be found by asking the group if anyone has experienced something similar, and allowing members to tell how they coped. These people are valuable resources to the group and to the leader.

Development of Socializing Techniques

Some psychoeducational groups have this factor as a goal; others may focus on it or emphasize it without stating it as a goal. It may be incidental for other groups; and for some it is unimportant. Where the factor is a goal or focus, the leader takes the responsibility for introducing the topic, attending to it, and recognizing it. When members learn a behavior and practice it in the group, the leader also provides reinforcement.

This factor, more than any other, provides you with opportunities to introduce and teach socializing techniques. These may be relating, communicating, or social skills, but all are designed to produce better interpersonal relations, reduce feelings of isolation and alienation, and promote self-confidence.

Even in groups for which development of socializing techniques is not a focus, or for which it is only incidental to the main goal, it still can be helpful. The leader needs to be alert to these opportunities and be prepared to capitalize on them. For example, the goal for the group or session may be on time management. Socializing techniques typically are not a part of the focus for this topic. However, telephone communication and manners may be on the agenda. It is then appropriate for you to introduce some socializing techniques and allow participants to discuss their problems or experiences. You may even build some awareness of transfer of learning to other situations.

Interpersonal Learning

Yalom (1985) described the interpersonal learning sequence this way: First, a behavior, usually a maladaptive or inappropriate behavior, is displayed. "Through feedback and self-observation, one (1) becomes a better observer of one's behavior; (2) appreciates the impact of that behavior upon (a) the feelings of others, (b) the opinions that others have of one, (c) the opinion one has of oneself."

Thus, it is through observation and constructive feedback that interpersonal learning takes place. For some members this may be the first time they have received constructive feedback that they can use. While this may not be enough to alter behavior significantly, it is the beginning of awareness that leads to significant change.

Interpersonal learning is not the focus for many psychoeducational groups, as it has an intense affective component that may not be appropriate for the group. Groups focused on study skills, time management, and meetings may not be appropriate forums for interpersonal learning to occur. While it is not impossible for this factor to emerge for some members, it is not the goal or emphasis. Other groups, such as conflict management, anger control, parenting, and support groups, may have interpersonal learning as an expectation and provide appropriate means for it to emerge, to be recognized, and to be capitalized upon.

Cohesiveness

It is not unusual for members of intact groups (e.g., a department) to be part of a psychoeducational group or to be the group. While there may or may not be group cohesiveness present simply from working together or having other common experiences, the group leader needs to be aware that some measure of cohesiveness may already be present. This may be both a plus and a minus.

Groups tend to become cohesive around perceived similarities. If group members already know their similarities, the leader does not need to point them out. The group has already moved toward cohesiveness.

The negative sides are that others in the group (those not from that department) may feel excluded, and the unit may form a clique within the group. If there is tension or dissension in the unit, it also may impact the functioning of the larger group.

One major issue experienced by members of all types of groups is inclusion versus exclusion. Although not expressed openly or directly, members want to know if they will be accepted by other members and by the leader. When there is already a subgroup that knows and accepts each other, other members wonder if that subgroup will dominate, leaving them out, or if the group will be structured to include the subgroup *and* other group members. Leaders who do not actively attend to this concern will not be able to develop cohesiveness, and group members will not feel positive about the group experience.

An even worse possibility for the group and leader is if the unit forms a clique within the group. Not only do other members feel excluded, the leader may find that control of the group has been assumed by the clique. More time and attention may be given to dealing with the clique, which takes away time needed for the topic and for other members.

The most destructive situation is if the unit has tension or dissension among its members. Sometimes the suppression of intense negative affect will have an effect on participants, and the leader and other members will not understand why the group is not going well. Everyone will leave feeling churned up, without a clue as to why they feel this way. Or, worse still, conflict will break out into the open and the leader's lack of knowledge of history, people, or issues will prevent successful intervention. In this case, the entire purpose of the group will be lost.

What about groups in which members do not have working or personal relationships prior to joining the group? Can cohesiveness be developed in these groups? The answer is yes: Some level of cohesiveness can be established even if the group life is only two to three hours. While this cohesiveness may be minimal, shared experiences in an atmosphere in which members feel safe, respected, and valued does produce cohesiveness. This is where the personal characteristics and skills of the leader are needed most: You will use those skills and characteristics to produce a situation in which cohesiveness (albeit minimal) can emerge.

FACTORS UNLIKELY TO APPEAR

Catharsis, corrective recapitulation of the family of origin, and existential factors are unlikely to appear in a manner that is useful to the goals of the psychoeducational group. The very experienced leader who has training in leading counseling/therapy groups may recognize the appearance of these factors. Leaders who do not have the training and experience are less likely to do so. These factors have their therapeutic value but probably cannot be successfully incorporated into psychoeducational groups.

Catharsis

Emotional venting together with intrapersonal learning describes catharsis. Most psychoeducational groups are not conducted to promote this kind of response; if emotional venting occurs, it may be destructive to the goals of the group and safety concerns of the members. There are psychoeducational groups in which some level of catharsis may occur: for example, anger management or conflict mediation. In these instance, the group leader should be trained in these areas and able to use the catharsis constructively. These groups typically run for several sessions, which allows safety and trust to be developed before catharsis appears.

Corrective Recapitulation of the Family of Origin

Recapitulation of the family of origin can be inferred from observation of group members' behavior over time. Most psychoeducational groups do not last long enough for the necessary observation, nor do most leaders have the needed training and experience. Further, this factor does not apply to the goals of most psychoeducational groups.

An additional component necessary for this to be a therapeutic factor is for the group and leader to make the recapitulation of the family of origin a corrective experience: that is, to help the member recognize his or her transferences and projections so that they will not affect relationships outside the family of origin. For example, if a group member is in conflict with authority figures, or with those perceived to be authority figures, being aware of the transference of feelings about a parent onto these figures can allow that member to understand his or her conflicts better and to make changes in behavior—seeing the person as he or she is, not in terms of past family relationships.

Existential Factors

Existential factors seem to be always present in some form; however, in order to be therapeutic, they must be dealt with on some level, and it is unlikely that they will occur in a manner relevant to the goals of psychoeducational groups. Further, a leader needs training and experience to recognize existential factors and to be confident of his or her ability to effectively deal with them.

Self-help groups are the only category of groups addressed in this book in which existential factors may be therapeutic. These groups tend to be long-term, focused on a particular issue, and more personal than task-oriented. They also tend not to have designated leaders, but a leader knowledgeable about existential factors can help the group make therapeutic use of such factors when they emerge.

Chapter 6

MANAGING CONFLICT AND GUIDELINES FOR CONFRONTING

Conflict can emerge in a group at any time—between members, between a member and the leader, or between the group and the leader. Conflict with others outside the group may be brought into the group and displaced onto members or the leader. There may be differences of opinion, personal animosities, defiance or rebellion against authority figures, or a general hostile attitude. Whatever the cause of the conflict, the leader must be prepared to handle it in ways that benefit members and facilitate the progress of the group.

Variable conflict management uses a multifaceted approach, taking into account the stage of group development and the maturity level of group members. This strategy can be used for most of the conflicts that commonly emerge.

Probably the most important components in managing conflict are the leader's abilities to tolerate ambiguity and anxiety, to anticipate and plan for managing conflicts, and in blocking and confrontation. The leader is in control and has the responsibility for constructively managing conflicts.

CHARACTERISTIC CONFLICT BEHAVIOR

Most discussions of conflict management list five characteristic ways people behave in conflicts: withdrawing, forcing, soothing, compromising, and confronting. The discussion that follows describes these behaviors and advantages and disadvantages of each. Leaders can and should use more than one conflict management strategy, but they also need to be aware of members' needs, outside forces, and the stage of group development.

Withdrawing

Withdrawing is defined as a physical or emotional retreat, a refusal to engage. The advantage of withdrawing is that the conflict ceases. The disadvantage is that the underlying issue, problem, or concern does not get addressed, and this strategy may leave residual uncomfortable feelings.

Forcing

Forcing is characteristic of individuals who must win at all costs. They attack, intimidate, and generally behave in a way that forces their point of view on others. Again, conflicts do not get worked out; the conflict also may escalate if others fight back or be suppressed if others withdraw.

Soothing

As a management strategy, soothing may keep the conflict from escalating or becoming more intense. The attempt to produce harmony can sometimes work if there are intense uncomfortable feelings involved. However, this strategy can be manipulative if the soother is meeting his or her own needs to reduce tension and not taking into account the needs of others to work through the conflict. For some, even a slight hint of conflict produces strong feelings based on childhood experiences, usually in the family, which leads to soothing behavior. There are other times when soothing is appropriate: for example, when a conflict cannot be worked through because intense feelings are involved or out of control. Participants may be able to work through the conflict if they are soothed to the point where they can each hear what the other is saying.

Compromising

Compromising takes place when both sides give up something to arrive at a resolution or solution. Negotiating takes skill and a willingness to meet the other person at least halfway. However, compromising assumes that both parties are willing to be involved in reaching a solution or resolution. One person in a conflict cannot compromise without the other. Some individuals perceive compromising as losing.

Confronting

Confronting is a skill that can be learned. It is not easy, especially since it has come to be synonymous with attack. Confrontation is an invitation to the other person to examine his or her behavior and its impact on you. It assumes there is a relationship to be preserved and that you want to preserve it. It is not an opportunity to dump on the other person all the negative thoughts and feelings you have experienced about them. Further, the other person does not have to accept the invitation. Confrontations are not forced on the other, they must be accepted. All of these characteristics limit the usefulness of confrontation as a conflict management strategy in psychoeducational groups.

VARIABLE CONFLICT MANAGEMENT STRATEGIES

Variable conflict management strategies (VCMS) include the five listed above, plus four other skills: distracting, ignoring, delaying, and holding firm.

Distracting

Distracting involves introducing a new topic, reframing, or refocusing on some other aspect of the conflict. Distracting may be useful if the leader does not want to withdraw or ignore the conflict, but instead redirects it to focus on something more useful. For example, the conflict may be a flare-up over some small event that does not have much to do with the task of the group. The leader can intervene and block an escalation of the conflict by introducing another topic.

Ignoring

Just as with children, it sometimes is better to ignore some conflicts. Some people use conflict as an attention-getting mechanism, and the leader can get sucked into dealing with the conflict instead of focusing on the task at hand. Learning to recognize when to ignore comes with experience.

Delaying

Delaying intervention to manage the conflict gives participants time to cool off. There may be times when the leader wants to teach positive conflict management skills or model them, but the intensity of feelings involved in the conflict makes it unwise to do so at that time. Some reasons for delaying include these: the group may choose sides, the differences may escalate, physical violence may ensue, or the emotional fragility of members may be such that working through the conflict at that moment would produce more disturbance for them. Delaying does not mean withdrawing from the conflict; it is a temporary disengagement.

Holding Firm

Holding firm is a conflict management strategy that is somewhat authoritarian in nature. The leader takes the responsibility for blocking behaviors that contribute to the conflict, stating rules and guidelines for participation by reminding participants of them and enforcing them).

In addition, VCMS use the status of group members on two dimensions: responsibility and expertise. The assumption behind VCMS is that the group leader needs to respond differently to conflicts in the group depending on the responsibility levels and expertise of the group members. Any one conflict management strategy may not fit the abilities of the group members. The expert group leader will be able to use the full range of conflict management strategies and to judge when and where to use each.

Another variable in deciding which strategy to use is knowing the kind of conflict involved: an individual group member's conflict with the leader, the group's conflict with the leader, conflicts among members, and conflicts between groups or cliques of members all require different management strategies. The leader must deal with each of these conflicts in different ways at different stages of the group, and also take into consideration the status of the members involved.

Levels of Responsibility and Expertise

Members will vary greatly in their degrees of responsibility and levels of expertise. These dimensions may be more important in terms of conflict management than age, gender, and education.

Responsibility. I take my definition of responsibility from the description of class II scales for the *California Psychological Inventory* (Gough, 1975). The scales measure socialization, maturity, responsibility, and intrapersonal structuring of values. The functions of the scales are

> to identify persons of conscientious, responsible, and dependable disposition and temperament; to indicate the degree of social maturity, integrity, and rectitude the individual has attained; to assess the degree and adequacy of self-regulation and self-control and freedom from impulsivity and self-centeredness; to identify personal with permissive, accepting and nonjudgmental social beliefs; and to identify persons capable of creating a favorable impression, and who are concerned about how others react to them. (p. 10)

While age plays a role in the degree of responsibility and maturity, this dimension is not totally age-related. The expectation for exhibition of responsibility is age-related in that one does not expect the same manifestation of responsibility from a child or adolescent that one does from an adult. Instead, it is reasonable to expect children and adolescents to manifest responsible behavior appropriate for their age level.

High-responsibility descriptors include cooperative, outgoing, sociable, warm, planning, capable, conscientious, and dependable. Low-responsibility descriptors include under-controlled and impulsive in behavior, defensive, opinionated, passive and overly judgmental in attitude, wary, and overemphasizing personal pleasure and self-gain.

Expertise. The dimension of expertise is defined with descriptors of communication skills, such as attending, ability to suspend judgment and listen to the other, focusing on issues, ability to tolerate ambiguity, and personal ownership of feelings and attitudes. Expertise is the dimension that can more easily be developed and forms the focus for some skills groups. When dealing with conflict in the group, the leader can evaluate the participants' expertise by observing interactions in the group.

MODEL FOR VCMS

The model in Table 6.1 categorizes participants' behavior into six categories using the dimensions of responsibility and expertise. A description of some behaviors illustrates each, and the nine management strategies are associated with each category of dimensions.

TABLE 6.1
Model for Management Strategies Based on Member Status

Status	Behavior	Strategy
Low responsibility and expertise	Unwilling & unable (defiant, hostile)	Holding firm
Low responsibility/ Moderate expertise	Tends to be unwilling but has some skills	Ignoring, distracting, delaying, confronting
Moderate responsibility/ Low expertise	Willing, but not knowledgeable	Delaying (leader), soothing, or withdrawing
Moderate responsibility/ Moderate expertise	Willing and able with sufficient support and encouragement	Compromising, confronting, or soothing
Moderate responsibility/ High expertise	Knows what and how to approach conflicts. May choose not to do so.	Compromising or confronting
High responsibility/ High expertise	Both willing and able	Withdrawing or confronting

Discription of Categories

Low Responsibility/Low Expertise. Participants in this category can be very difficult, especially if they are also involuntary participants. They are both unwilling to trust and cooperate, and unable to adequately attend to the task. The group leader may experience them as being sullen and hostile. Conflicts involving these participants need to be handled with clear, firm directions that remind them what the expected behaviors are and just what will, and will not, be tolerated.

Low Responsibility/Moderate Expertise. This category includes participants who are not as difficult to deal with as the previous category as they have some skills and could attend to the task but appear to be unwilling to do so. They would be described as immature for their age. While these participants also profit from clear, firm guidelines, their conflicts can be managed with ignoring, distracting, and delaying.

Moderate Responsibility/Low Expertise. These participants are willing to be cooperative and try to accomplish the task, but they lack the knowledge and the skills that would enable them to do so. The group leader who assumes that, because these participants are cooperating, they can do what is required to meet the groups goals will be very disappointed when he or she realizes that the participants simply do no know how to accomplish what needs to be done. Conflict management strategies that are useful here include confronting, delaying, and soothing.

Moderate Responsibility/Moderate Expertise.   These are the participants who are willing, have the necessary knowledge and skills, but need encouragement and support to carry out the task. They need reassurance that they are doing what is needed and will respond to encouragement. The group leader can use withdrawing, compromising, confronting, and soothing as conflict management strategies.

Moderate Responsibility/High Expertise.   The participants in this category are very able to accomplish the task. They have the knowledge and skills but, for one reason or the other, may choose not to use them constructively. The conflict management strategies that work best with them are compromising and confronting.

High Responsibility/High Expertise.   These are the ideal participants who have both the sense of responsibility and the needed expertise. The group leader may need to withdraw and let them handle the conflict or confront if they do not seem to be on the right track.

An Example

A brief scenario is presented below that shows behaviors representative of each category, along with a leader response that illustrates four of the suggested variable conflict management strategies.

> Two members get into a heated argument over a minor point. Their voices get louder, their fists clench, and their facial expressions are angry.

Holding Firm Response.   "I am going to break into the discussion here and remind members of the agreement we all made to maintain respect for differing points of view. We can continue to discuss this point if you like. However, all group members must take part in the discussion, and respect for one another must be demonstrated. Or I can address the point in question and make a decision. Which do you prefer?"

Distracting Response. "I wonder if you two can hold off presenting your points of view until the group deals with _____? I promise that we will get back to them."

Soothing Response. "I can see that both of you feel strongly about this issue. It would be helpful if each of you would help me and the other members understand your point and its importance to you. If you agree, you can present your viewpoint one at a time. We'll go in alphabetical order by last name."

Confronting Response. "Your argument is affecting group members, and I can see that they are uncomfortable. I feel somewhat uncomfortable as well, as you both seem ready to have a physical fight. I wonder if it is possible for us to discuss the disputed point with you?"

This is an example of a conflict between group members. The specific responses would be different when dealing with other types of conflicts.

CONFRONTATION

Confrontation can be negative and destructive or positive and constructive. Often it is perceived only as negative, destructive, and aggressive because the term is used improperly and the purpose is misunderstood. Confrontation is *not* synonymous with aggression, and it should not be used to accomplish these purposes:

- telling people off,

- attacking,

- browbeating others to get them to see your point or agree with you,

- criticism,

- one-upmanship,

- for someone's "own good,"

- to be perceived as "right," and

- for vindication.

These are harmful motives, and they will promote feelings of hostility and defensiveness in others. In order for relationships to grow, develop, and become strong, confrontation should be a positive and constructive interaction. "Confrontation is an invitation to an individual to examine his or her behavior and its consequences or impact on others" (Egan, 1975).

Major Types of Confrontation

Berenson, Mitchell, and Laney (1968) identified five major types of confrontation: didactic, experiential, weakness, strength, and encouragement to action. Each approaches the invitation to examine behavior in a different way, and all are constructive when used appropriately.

Didactic.   Didactic confrontation assumes the receiver lacks important information or has misunderstood the information; in this case the confrontation is used to remedy the condition. Didactic confrontation, however, involves more than simply giving information. The receiver is asked to examine his or her behavior and how it may be affecting the confronter because of faulty perceptions or ignorance.

An example of didactic confrontation would be if a member insisted that the group end at 4 P.M. when the scheduled time for ending was 5 P.M. After correcting the misinformation, the leader could explore the impact of early termination on the process.

Experiential.   Experiential confrontation is so named because there is a significant difference in how the receiver perceives him- or herself and how you perceive him or her. This is particularly useful when the receiver has a distorted (either positive or negative) perception of him- or herself and does not see the impact of his or her behavior on others because of the misperception. The confronter shares how he or she experiences the receiver, and how this perception appears to differ from that which the receiver has of him- or herself.

For example: A group member says that he finds it difficult to express anger. Other members confront by saying that this is not how they have experienced him. They note that he has been open in expressing irritation and annoyance, and the openness has been appreciated because they did not have to try to guess his feelings.

Weakness.   In weakness confrontation, the focus is on the receiver's deceits or inadequacies. A weakness confrontation is not an attack or a put-down, but an invitation to the receiver to examine these weaknesses and how they influence his or her relationships.

For example, asking a member to examine how she continually interrupts others, and the impact that has on communications and relationships, is a weakness confrontation.

Strength. Strength confrontations, on the other hand, ask the receiver to look at underused or overlooked resources, assets, or strengths. This can be a particularly positive and powerful confrontation, as the receiver gains more awareness of heretofore hidden resources.

For example, in a strength confrontation, the group might point out to a member that he has been persistent in the face of many obstacles and then list instances of that persistence.

Encouragement to Action. The encouragement to action confrontation supports the receiver in taking an action instead of reacting passively. Many times individuals know what would be beneficial for them but lack the resolve to take action. Confronting them with encouragement and support can give them the confidence to move forward.

Kurtz and Jones (1973) found that strength and encouragement to action confrontations are most positively received and acted on. The least effective confrontations are didactic and weakness. Didactic can easily become lectures, and weakness confrontations can be perceived as criticizing and faultfinding. These should be used with caution.

Guidelines for Confronting

The group leader needs to consider several things before a confrontation: the purpose of the group, the extent of safety and trust developed in the group and with members, the type of conflict, the current psychological state of members and of the group as a whole, expectation of change in behavior, personal motives for confronting, and the rationale for confronting.

Purpose of the Group. Before confronting, you must consider the purpose of the group. If it is a skills learning group, the confrontation may be appropriate for modeling and learning. If, on the other hand, it is more of a class than a group, you may be better off not engaging in confrontation. The question you must ask yourself is this: Will the confrontation help the group and its members? If the answer is not an unqualified "yes," you should not use the confrontation.

Established Safety and Trust. Confronting before adequate safety and trust have been established in the group produces a lot of anxiety. Other members may fear that they, too, will be confronted and so restrict their input. Confronting too early can put a damper on the group and cause more resistance.

Type of Conflict. The type of conflict also plays a part in deciding when or whether to confront. Is the conflict between members? Should they be given a chance to work it out before you intervene? Is the conflict between the group and you? This is expected at some point and may not need a confrontation; it might instead call for another kind of response. Is the conflict one in which most of the group is in agreement and in conflict with one member? Is it scapegoating? Should it be blocked or confronted? Is the conflict between you and one member? Will a confrontation be perceived as a power struggle or as an attack on the member? These are not easy questions, but they should be considered before you engage in a confrontation.

Psychological States of Group Members. You must consider the psychological state of the member and of the group before embarking on a confrontation. If there is a great deal of intense emotion involved, the confrontation should be delayed or discarded. If the member or the group is in a fragile state, the confrontation may not be appropriate. The receiver of the confrontation must be able to hear what is said and meant, and also be able to use it.

Willingness to Consider Changing. Confrontations are invitations to examine behavior, and the receiver should be left free to decide whether or not to use the information. However, if you do not have a realistic expectation that a positive behavioral change will result, the confrontation is counterproductive. You must ask yourself if the receiver is willing to change. If the answer is "no," you should not confront.

Leader's Motives. Your motives for confronting also play a part in your decision. Indeed, they are crucial. You should never confront if your motive is to maintain control, to exert power or domination, to manipulate, to attack or take revenge, to punish, to show off your expertise, or as vindication.

Rationale for Confronting. All positive purposes for confronting are related to promoting development of the individual or the group. Confrontation may be aimed at giving the receiver more direct awareness of his or her behavior and its consequences. Confrontation can provide additional perspectives if validated by other group members. It can provide an opportunity for safe self-examination, self-exploration, and behavior change. Positive confrontations can strengthen relationships.

Confronter, Receiver, and Condition Variables

In every confrontation, there are three distinct, dynamic variables: the confronter, the receiver of the confrontation, and the conditions surrounding the confrontation. Each of these variables must be examined *before the confrontation* if it is to be a positive experience.

Confronter Variables. Before any confrontation, you should examine the following variables.

> **The emotional state of the confronter:** Confrontations are most effective if the confronter is calm, empathetic, accepting, and caring.

> **The motives or reasons for the confrontation:** The confronter must be aware of his or her rationale for the confrontation. If the confronter is unsure or confused about those reasons, the confrontation should be delayed or discarded.

> **The ability to distinguish clearly between facts and feelings:** Confrontations are most effective when the confronter can identify feelings as feelings and facts as facts. Awareness of and sensitivity to the relationship is also a component: What kind and level of relationship exists between the confronter and receiver? Are you seeking to strengthen the relationship? Do you care about the relationship? The confronter's feelings about and expectations for the relationship are vital components in the decision to confront.

Receiver Variables. You also must consider several things about the receiver of the confrontation, including these:

> **The receiver's emotional state:** Individuals under the influence of intense emotions are less likely to be open to confrontation. It is better to wait and confront when emotions are less intense.

> **The receiver's capacity for self-examination:** Individuals who are closed to self-examination or who deny the need for self-examination cannot be confronted with positive results.

The degree of trust the receiver has in the confronter: If the person being confronted does not trust the confronter to be genuine or to have positive regard for him or her, the confrontation will not be perceived as justified, correct, or necessary.

Condition Variables. Conditions surrounding the confrontation play an important role in determining how the confrontation is received. The primary considerations are circumstances and timing:

Audience: Who beside the confronter and the receiver is present? There are times when the support of others can be helpful, if the others reinforce the confronting statements. If, however, the relationships are not trusting, accepting, or caring, then the presence of others can be perceived as "ganging up."

Environmental conditions: Social gatherings, meetings, or family reunions are not appropriate venues for positive confrontations. Being sensitive to the purpose of the setting can make a difference in whether the confrontation is successful.

Fundamentals of Confronting

Once the decision to confront has been made, the confronter should keep some communication fundamentals in mind, including the following:

1. Use a positive approach.

2. Choose words that suit the receiver's emotional state.

3. Be concrete; say what's on your mind.

4. Be aware of the impact you are having on the receiver.

5. Wait for a response or reaction.

6. Be sure of your facts.

7. Do not exaggerate or make broad generalizations.

8. Think before you speak.

9. Check to ensure that you are being understood accurately.

10. Stick to the topic; do not bring in other concerns or issues.

11. Try not to criticize.

12. Do not impose your views, just express them.

13. Be receptive to feedback.

14. Listen to the other person.

15. Do not interrupt.

16. Give people the time they need to absorb the information.

SUMMARY OF CONSTRUCTIVE CONFRONTATION

You should approach confrontation as you would positive feedback. Use some of the same criteria and assumptions to promote constructive reception of the confrontation. Below are some suggestions for increasing the probability of a positive, constructive confrontation.

Make your statements descriptive, not evaluative. Describing the behavior is objective; making judgments about the behavior is subjective. The more objective you can be, the more apt everyone is to agree that this is, in fact, the observed behavior.

Focus on a specific behavior rather than being general in your description. It is not helpful to use terms that are ambiguous and do not describe a specific behavior: For example, telling someone he or she is domineering is not concrete or helpful. However, telling someone that he or she has been interrupting the conversation often, and then giving examples, is specific. In addition, do not infer motives for the behavior. This is speculative and must be inferred, making it subjective and part of one's personal experience. It also raises the possibility that others will not agree, as their experiences may have been different.

Remember that the needs of the receiver are more important than the needs of the confronter. This is a sensitive and risky undertaking, which may be very threatening for the receiver. While you as confronter may undergo some of the same feelings, *you are the initiator*. Be tentative and ready to stop at any time if the receiver appears overwhelmed.

Wait for an invitation to confront. Confrontation is most useful and constructive if it is solicited rather than imposed. Asked-for confrontations generally mean that the receiver is willing and able to use the feedback and feels a need to get some. However, it takes a long time for relationships to develop to the point where confrontations are actively sought. You may wish to use moderate confrontations even if they are not solicited.

Time your confrontations well. Timing is critical. Feedback is most useful when given close to the time of the behavior. If it is not possible to give the feedback at that time, wait until the behavior occurs again, delay, or discard it. If the receiver is in an emotional state that is not conducive to receiving the feedback, if other activities intervene, or if it is time to break or stop, the confrontation should be delayed or discarded.

Be prepared to listen, as confrontation involves sharing of information. Confrontation is not a *telling to* the receiver, it is a *dialogue*. Listening also gives cues as to the emotional state of the receiver, which tells you when to back off and when to continue.

As part of the listening, the feedback should be checked to ensure clear communication. Did the receiver hear what you said, or was it distorted in some way? Did you say what you intended to say, or was it different? It is easy for feedback under these conditions to be misunderstood.

Attend to the consequences of the feedback. Pay attention to the impact of your words on the receiver and on other group members. Remember that the confrontation will affect all group members in some way, not just the receiver.

Chapter 7

THE GROUP

GROUP DYNAMICS

Group dynamics refers to the ongoing process in the group. The shifting, changing, individual, and group-as-a-whole variables, including level of participation, resistance, communication patterns, relationships between members and between members and the leader, nonverbal behaviors, feeling tone, and feelings aroused and/or expressed.

Discussing individual dynamics does not allow you to understand the range and intensity, as the dynamics do not take place in the group one at a time. Group dynamics are continually and constantly interacting throughout the session, shifting emphasis, changing even as you observe them, and all are important in understanding what is happening in the group. However, the dynamics do have to be individually defined and described. Following are brief descriptions to help you observe group dynamics, along with a summary of focal dynamics for each stage of group development.

Level of Participation

The extent to which participants cooperate, interact with each other and with the leader, contribute to the progress and functioning of the group, and seek to gain knowledge from the experiences determines their levels of participation. How do members participate? Are they active, passive, sullen, reluctant, or withdrawn? Does their involvement change significantly at some point? For example, do they become energized or fall silent after a discussion? Observing these kinds of behaviors helps you gauge the needs of participants, the intensity of emotions aroused, and the impact of the group and of particular experiences.

Resistance

You should expect resistance, which will range from mild to intense. The presence of an observable resistance is a clear signal to move on to another person or topic. If the entire group is resisting, you may need to explore with members some of the reasons for the resistance. For example, if members do not want to do a particular exercise or activity, you can initiate a discussion on their perception of the usefulness of the activity. Simply asking what about the activity is a turn-off can produce some valuable information.

Communication Patterns

Members will communicate primarily to and through the leader, especially in the beginning. You can facilitate member-to-member communication by suggesting that members talk to each other directly rather than through you.

Another pattern to observe is this: Some members talk to and support each other, while other members are excluded. You can help bring excluded members into the group by asking for their input.

How communications take place is an additional pattern to watch over time; you cannot judge it by one incident. Do group members communicate in a warm, caring, supportive way? Or are communications cold, hostile, or angry? Do members appear wary, aloof, or tentative when they communicate? Individual patterns as well as group patterns should be observed.

Relationships

You should notice how members relate to each other and to you. Even groups whose members are not strangers to each other may be tentative at first and focus more on differences than on similarities.

The leader usually is perceived as "the expert" at the beginning. Members will expect you to provide for all their unspoken needs and expectations. Sometimes members will seek and compete for your attention and approval.

You can work on helping members establish relationships with each other and empower them to take charge and contribute to their own learning instead of looking to you to provide everything.

Nonverbal Behaviors

Postures, gestures, voice tones, and other nonverbal behaviors provide significant clues to what members are experiencing; these nonverbal signals are called *metacommunication*. Metacommunication is generally thought to be a more accurate reflection of a person's internal state than his or her verbal communication. For example, a person's words and voice may sound calm, but his or her tense posture, narrowed eyes, and clenched fists contradict the words.

Feeling Tone

You can get a good idea of how well the group is progressing by tuning in to the *feeling tone* of the group. This calls for a high level of self-awareness on your part as you must listen to what you are feeling as a possible reflection of what the group is feeling. Chapter 3 addresses the development of self-awareness in leaders.

Feelings Aroused/Expressed

Feelings aroused may be directly or indirectly expressed or they may be suppressed. A leader should be alert to feelings that are expressed in indirect ways, especially intense ones, as well as taking care to respond to directly expressed feelings. Suppressed feelings may be more troubling in some respects, but psychoeducational groups generally are not expected to deal with these. It is more appropriate that suppressed feelings be addressed in a counseling or therapy group.

GROUP STAGES

While group stages are defined somewhat differently by the experts (Bion, 1961; Yalom, 1985), it is commonly accepted that groups do move through stages. Two of these stages are obvious: beginning and termination. Others are not as easy to identify. These tend to be labeled the conflict and working stages.

Counseling and therapy groups are structured in such a way (e.g., a number of sessions held over time) that all the stages that are expected usually occur and are important in determining interventions for the group leader. These stages also occur for psychoeducational groups, although the indices of group stages are manifested in different and less intense ways.

Each of these stages is described in the following pages, along with some primary issues for each, expected member behaviors that illustrate basic issues, and suggestions for the leader. The emphasis is on the psychoeducational group, whether it consists of one session or many. Longer-term groups, for example, skill development, also will be addressed.

Stage 1. Beginning

The first stage for psychoeducational groups can be characterized by a sense of anticipation, excitement, dread, confusion, and apprehension. Even if there is to be little or no personal disclosure in the group, participants are not sure what they can expect or what is expected of them. Members want to know if they will be valued and included, or if they will be devalued and excluded. There are several steps you can take to reduce some of the negative feelings members bring to the group; however, no matter what you do, you will not be able to eliminate negative feelings altogether. You can expect these every time you begin a group.

The most useful step you can take to alleviate discomfort and uneasiness is to plan ahead carefully. Make sure that the facilities are adequate, that materials and supplies are on hand, that a schedule and agenda are prepared, and that you begin on time. Organized pscyhoeducational groups promote feelings of safety and trust.

The next step is to have an opening session that welcomes participants, introduces the personnel who will be working with the groups, and thoroughly reviews the objectives and schedule. Opening the dialogue to suggestions from participants also is useful. You should ask if the stated objectives meet the participants' expectations and needs, and if there are other topics or activities they want included.

The leader's listening, questioning, and facilitating skills make the difference in how the group gets off the ground. These topics will be covered more completely in chapter 3.

Stage 2. Conflict and Controversy

The second stage usually begins with an attack on the leader. This attack generally is so indirect that you may miss it. It is not important for you to recognize the attack as such; it is important that you not become defensive or retaliate. If you find yourself feeling defensive, explaining your rationale, reiterating something you thought was understood, or feeling that participants are being unfair, you probably are being attacked. There is no need to point this out, as it is unlikely that the group has moved to the level of development where they can accept your observation without feeling attacked themselves.

Another way the second stage is recognized is by the conflict that emerges between group members. If the group is on its way toward becoming more cohesive, then conflict will emerge; how you deal with such conflict will determine if the group continues to grow. Strategies for managing conflict are discussed in chapter 6.

Stage 3. Working and Cohesion

The working stage is characterized by cooperation and cohesiveness. Members are interested in and supportive of one another. They also are willing to work on a task and not become sidetracked. Issues that emerge at this stage have more to do with working through misunderstandings and differences of opinion and maintaining relationships than with winning/losing, saving face, and avoiding conflict.

Stage 4. Termination

The one stage that is denied but cannot be avoided is termination. Groups, especially psychoeducational groups, do come to an end. Members who are achieving their goals are reluctant to deal with ending and may refuse to discuss it at all. You should introduce the notion of termination some time before it happens. For example, in a one-day workshop termination would be introduced after lunch or before the afternoon break. Reminding participants of how much time is left and asking how would they like to use the time productively is one way of introducing the topic. The usual response is to change the subject or to move off it in some way. Bring the topic up again when there is about an hour left in the workshop, and plan a summary or wrap-up session. Some groups may want to help plan how they will terminate.

One issue around termination is the leader's response. Leaders, too, deny and avoid dealing with termination. They may end the group or session, but they do not terminate. Termination is an opportunity to tie up loose ends, express suppressed feelings, and work out troubling relationships. A satisfactory termination allows participants and the leader to end and leave without residual feelings of things left undone or "unfinished business."

Table 7.1 presents behaviors representative of each dynamic for four different stages of a group. Table 7.2 presents examples of themes and behaviors for different stages of a group.

TABLE 7.1
Dynamics and Group Stages for Psychoeducational Groups

Dynamics	Sample Expected Behaviors
Stage 1	
Level of Participation	Tentative, cautious, anxious; may engage in storytelling
Resistance	Usually high until safety is established. Ask many questions, appear or say they are confused
Communication Patterns	Most communication is to and through the leader. Member do not talk directly to each other but to the group, to the leader, or to no one in particular. Tend not to make "I" statements.
Member-to-Member Relationships	Tentative, polite, cautious, Fear of hurting others and of being hurt, fear of being different. Tend to focus on differences but search for similarities. Try to relate through advice-giving.
Member-to-Leader Relationships	Respectful; see leader as the expert, the magician. Expect leader to anticipate and meet their personal needs. Want to be reassured that they are valued and accepted by the leader. Want to know they are safe and will be taken care of.
Nonverbal Behaviors	Fluctuate for individual members between lots of movement (nervous) to little or no movement (tense). There may be little eye contact between members; closed gestures, such as arms folded across chest, backward

	lean; and few attending behaviors. Speech may be rapid, or slow and tentative.
Group Feeling Tone	The overall feeling tone from group members may range from apprehension to resentment, hostility, and despair. Usually, members leave with a sense of relief and hopefulness. Many feelings are experienced by members during these first sessions, but the overall feeling tone reflects the confusion, ambiguity, and frustration of group members as well as the changes induced by the leader's interventions.
Feelings Aroused/Expressed	Members will be somewhat reluctant to openly express feelings. Rather, they tend to try to suppress or deny them. This behavior affects the functioning of the group. Common feelings experienced are fear of rejection, fear of engulfment, fear of destruction, fear of shameful secrets, confusion, frustration. The leader's behavior can contribute to feelings of hopefulness, being cared for and valued, having something of value to contribute to the group.

Stage 2

Level of Participation	Increasing participation by members, a willingness to explore personal issues on a deeper but still superficial level, and more interaction between members.
Resistance	There is still considerable resistance, especially to being present-centered. Storytelling abounds with little or no recognition of commonalities between members. Members are also resistant to group-as-a-whole process commentary and may tend to personalize comments.
Communication Patterns	Members begin to talk directly to each other. Communication through the leader to the group and speaking for the group are reduced behaviors. Members begin to make supportive statements to each other and to challenge each other.
Member-to-Member Relationships	Conflict emerges in the group. Members feel safe enough to challenge each other and to report their feelings of anger or irritation. Past experiences with each other are revisited, projections and transference become more apparent.

Table 7.1 continued

Dynamics	Sample Expected Behaviors
Member-to-Leader Relationships	The leader is attacked by members. He or she has failed to be the "magician" or "expert" and members feel the loss of that idealization. The members still expect the leader to take care of them but are more willing to make their needs and desires known.
Nonverbal Behaviors	Members' postures and gestures are less studied and contrived. They appear to be willing to let their nonverbal communication be more consistent or congruent with their verbal behavior. The leader can tune in to nonverbal communication because members are more genuine.
Group Feeling Tone	Members are combative and irritable, producing a group feeling tone that is uncomfortable. Some members may fear conflict because of past experiences; when conflict emerges, they may regress to old feelings associated with conflicts for them. If conflicts are worked through constructively, the feeling tone becomes one of relief, having a sense of accomplishment, and hopefulness.
Feelings Aroused/Expressed	Irritation, annoyance, anger, rage, fear, guilt, are common feelings that arise and are expressed in this stage.
Stage 3	
Level of Participation	Members' levels of participation are high and significant personal issues emerge and are worked through.
Resistance	Resistance is more openly acknowledged, worked through, and understood by members and the leader. Members are more accepting of comments about perceived resistance.
Communication Patterns	Considerable member-to-member interaction. Cliques and subgroupings may be prevalent. The group functions more as a cohesive unit.
Member-to-Member Relationships	Members are more willing to explore relationships with each other. They will work to develop and maintain relationships, to the extent that conflicts may be minimized. When

	conflict does emerge it can be worked on or through in constructive ways.
Member-to-Leader Relationships	The leader is perceived as a guide and consultant, not as a magician or expert.
Nonverbal Behaviors	Members are much more congruent in nonverbal behaviors and verbal communications
Group Feeling Tone	Warm, accepting, a spirit of cooperation and satisfaction, excitement.
Feelings Aroused/Expressed	Irritation, annoyance, caring, warmth, liking, excitement at accomplishments, anticipation of continued learning about self, shame, guilt.

Stage 4

Level of Participation	Reduced or frantic participation. May withdraw or bring up new material, may end participating before the group ends (premature termination).
Resistance	Renewed resistance; this time to experiencing feelings around termination; either holding on or letting go.
Communication Patterns	Members talk to each other, but communication may revert to occurring through the leader.
Member-to-Member Relationships	Members begin to pull back from investing in relationships that may be ending. The quality and quantity of member relationships will change after termination.
Member-to-Leader Relationship	May be a realization of the value of the leader, an awareness of what he or she contributed, or a feeling of deprivation at the loss of the person and relationship; can be experienced as anger, annoyance, sadness.
Nonverbal Behaviors	Failure to maintain eye contact; looking at the floor, ceiling, or away from leader and members; shifting in seat; gathering possessions.
Group Feeling Tone	Sadness, relief.
Feelings Aroused/Expressed	Appreciation, pleasure, sadness, relief, abandonment, loss, grief.

TABLE 7.2
Stages of Group and Members' Behaviors

Major Themes	Expected Behaviors
Formative Stages	
Orientation	Search for similarities
Hesitant participation	Giving and seeking advice
Search for meaning	Symptom description
Dependency	Questions about value of experience
Safety	Leader seen as "all knowing"
	Desire for acceptance and approval, respect and domination
	Need for an omnipotent, omniscient, all-caring parent
Conflict	Conflicts between members
Dominance	Conflicts between members and leader
Rebellion	Negative comments
	Intermember criticism
	One-way analyses and judgments
	"Shoulds" and "oughts"
	Jockeying for position
	Hostility toward the leader
	Discounting of leader's expertise
Working Stages	
Cohesiveness	Increased morale
	Mutual trust
	Self-disclosure
	Intimacy develops
	May suppress negative affect
Working through process	Subgrouping may appear
	Conflict expresses as
	a. mutual contempt
	b. self-contempt
	c. transference
	d. mirroring
	e. projective identification
	f. rivalry
Working through process	Self-disclosure
	a. appropriate
	b. inappropriate
Terminating Stage	
Termination	Ignoring the impending end of group
	Denying feelings around the ending of group
	Unresolved issues around separation

DEVELOPING THE GROUP

Pregroup Planning

Planning a psychoeducational group is a developmental process in which the leader's professional preparation and skill provide a basis on which the group is built. Knowledge of theory and techniques, skill in facilitation, and proficiency in the subject matter are all prerequisites for successful psychoeducational groups.

Several factors should be considered prior to developing strategies. The overall goals and objectives for the group should be established. Simply having a topic is not enough. The leader must have a clear goal for the group from which strategies will be developed. Another crucial factor relates to participants' characteristics. Characteristics such as age, educational level, maturity, readiness, and kind of participation (voluntary or involuntary) are significant in deciding on goals and objectives. Related to these variables are ethical issues and therapeutic factors, which are discussed more fully in chapter 5.

Regardless of the topic, the group leader should research the latest literature in the field. Expertise is developed by constantly increasing one's knowledge and skill, not by sitting back and assuming one knows all there is to know about a topic. There may not be significant new information, but that should be checked and not assumed.

Setting Goals, Objectives, and Strategies

Reasonable goals and objectives contribute to feelings of accomplishment because they can be achieved. Try not to set goals that are so broad that there is little likelihood of achieving them. Both you and the participants will be frustrated if none of their goals is achieved in some measure. Generally, there is one goal for the group and several objectives. Objectives are manageable parts of the broader goal. They also point out steps needed to reach the goal.

You may use several strategies to attain an objective. For example, an objective for a time management seminar could be to increase awareness of personal time wasters. Strategies might include a mini-lecture identifying personal time wasters, a paper-and-pencil activity that reviews a day or the previous week, and brainstorming in small groups to develop suggestions for reducing personal time wasters.

Participants' Characteristics

You probably will know a few characteristics about the potential partici-pants in an upcoming group. The most significant are age range and educa-tional levels. If the group is being held for a particular group—for example, an agency—you also may know the occupations of the participants. One way you can obtain more inferred information about participants is to write a descrip-tion of the intended audience in the flyer or brochure announcing the group. It probably is safe to assume that those who choose to attend the group meet the description fairly well.

Just knowing the age range and educational levels will help you set goals and objectives and select strategies. Words and concepts chosen for mini-lec-tures and reading materials, the degree of complexity for directions, and the time frame for activities can be better determined knowing these two partici-pant characteristics.

Instructional Strategies

Learning theory, instructional principles, and participants' characteristics interact when selecting instructional strategies. Knowing what is effective for learning, retention, and transfer as well as the expected maturity and readiness levels will help you choose effective instructional strategies. Distribution of practice and learning, building on previous knowledge, and most effective meth-ods also contribute.

There are four general categories of instructional strategies: passive (e.g., lectures and use of media), active verbal (e.g., discussions, forms, and role-play), active combined verbal and nonverbal (e.g., exercises and games), and active nonverbal (e.g., movement). There is some overlap between categories, such as when discussion is used after an exercise. Your choice of instructional strategies for psychoeducational groups should emphasize active methods. In-structional strategies are discussed in more detail in chapter 2.

Sample Plan.   What follows is an example of how setting the goal and objectives can help a leader select strategies for a psychoeducational group on time management for secretaries in a human services agency. The participants are expected to be between the ages of 18 and 60, with educational levels rang-ing from a high school diploma to a community college degree. They will be primarily female. The group will meet for six hours in a one-day session.

TABLE 7.3
Sample Objectives and Strategies

Objective	Strategies
Participants will:	
1. Develop an awareness of the importance of daily planning	1. Mini-lecture on advantages of planning daily
2. Learn the ABC method for prioritizing tasks	2. Game: Participants will make a "to do" list for the following day and prioritize the tasks, giving the most important tasks an A, etc.
3. Learn the role of short-term and long-term goals	3. Participants fill out the form on setting goals and discuss their responses in small groups
4. Learn the effectiveness of working on important tasks rather than time-consuming unimportant tasks	4. Mini-lecture on distinguishing between categories of tasks: urgent but not important; important but not urgent; urgent and important; neither urgent nor important
5. Learn a method for managing large, involved tasks, such as reports	5. Present Larkin's Swiss cheese method for large tasks.

Goal: Participants will learn time management strategies that can be applied to their work setting.

Forming Small Groups

Many psychoeducational groups include large numbers of participants. Active participation is enhanced when the participants can interact in small groups. Forming small groups can be accomplished in several ways. The most simple and efficient way is preassigning members to small groups: The leader simply decides how many members will be in each group, divides the participants by that number, and assigns them to groups by colors, by numbers, or by some other designation. Their group designations can then be put on participants' name tags or on the folders given to them when they first come to the session.

Another way to make small group assignments is to decide on the number of small groups you want, and then have participants count off by that number.

This is more time-consuming, however, and can be confusing for participants if the group numbers more than 35.

The most inefficient method is to let participants choose their own small groups. This usually results in friends choosing the same group and perhaps forming a clique. This procedure can result in uneven numbers for groups as well, with some having few members and others having more than can be comfortably accommodated.

Materials

You should put as many materials as possible into the package participants receive as they enter the session. It is helpful if the packages can be put on chairs or tables before the session. Trying to hand them out at the door while giving participants name tags and taking roll or collecting money produces bottlenecks.

Prepare handouts and other materials so that they can be easily read and handled. Have extra copies of everything in case additional materials are needed.

It is more time-consuming to hand out materials in a large group, even when assistance is available. Try to place materials for small groups in the rooms or at the tables where groups will be working.

If participants are expected to write or draw, tables are essential. The best room layout provides tables for five to seven participants each. Individual desks are inefficient and provide barriers to small group discussion.

Break-out rooms for small groups provide privacy and minimize the impact of environmental disruptions. When facilities do not allow for break-out rooms, the room must be large enough to allow for separation of small groups.

Facilities should be clean, with adequate lighting and climate control. Restrooms and water fountains should be easily accessible.

EVALUATING THE GROUP

There are several ways to obtain feedback for evaluative purposes, including discussion, survey or rating forms, attitude and behavioral ratings. All have advantages and disadvantages.

Discussion provides the most immediate feedback and promotes personal ownership of opinions. The primary disadvantages are that time typically permits only a few participants to give input, and many people are reluctant to openly verbalize their opinions.

Survey or rating forms allow all participants to have input and also focus input on those parts of the group where feedback is desired. A disadvantage of survey or rating forms is that participants may limit their input to answering the form's questions.

Attitude and behavioral scales usually are commercial in nature and, in addition to the cost, may have limited or questionable validity and reliability. Selecting appropriate instruments requires a knowledge of psychometry.

The best way to evaluate a psychoeducational group—and to receive information that can help you in making modifications, revisions, or a change of direction—is to use a form tailored for your specific group. I encourage you either to learn more about constructing evaluation materials or to consult with someone who is knowledgeable in the field and have him or her develop the form.

Planning for Evaluation

Planning for evaluation begins before the group ever meets. Evaluation is not an add-on, it is an integral part of the planning process. Deciding what information you want, planning for when and how to collect it, and selecting suitable instrumentation will help you prepare for effective evaluation.

Evaluating Goals, Objectives, and Strategies

One way to begin the process is to list the group's objectives and strategies, then tie these to the method of evaluation. For example, one objective may be to have participants learn a body of material. The strategy to be used is a mini-lecture. Evaluation of learning might include having participants take a test, brainstorm or write applications of the material, rate the presentation, or judge their impression of how much they learned. You could also use pre- and posttesting to determine gains in learning.

Listing objectives and strategies also allows for prioritizing, so that you evaluate what is most important and you don't waste time overevaluating. It is

TABLE 7.4
Sample Evaluation Form

Study Skills Group

I. **Directions:** Rate how useful you feel each of the following will be to you in improving your study skills. Write comments in the space provided.

   5 = extremely useful   2 = somewhat useful

   4 = very useful   1 = not useful to me

   3 = useful

   1. Handouts   5   4   3   2   1

   Comments:_____

   2. Lecture/discussion   5   4   3   2   1

   Comments:_____

   3. Exercise (Setting goals)   5   4   3   2   1

   Comments:_____

II. **Directions:** Rate each of the items below using the following scale:

   5 = extremely useful   2 = somewhat useful

   4 = very useful   1 = not useful to me

   3 = useful

	5	4	3	2	1
4. Organization of the information and of the group	5	4	3	2	1
5. Quality or interest of the presentation(s)	5	4	3	2	1
6. The leader's preparation, enthusiasm, and delivery	5	4	3	2	1
7. Opportunities for input or interaction	5	4	3	2	1
8. Facilities	5	4	3	2	1
9. Schedule: events, breaks, etc.	5	4	3	2	1
10. Overall quality	5	4	3	2	1

not necessary or desirable to evaluate everything in-depth. Instead, focus on the important elements and plan a short evaluation. Sometimes all you need is feedback on participants' perception of the major activities. A simple form listing these, a method for rating them, and space for written comments may suffice. For example, a half-day psychoeducational group on study skills that used an icebreaker, handouts, a mini-lecture, and an exercise could use a form similar to the one in Table 7.4. (Note: More space would be provided for comments.)

The form in Table 7.4 provides for rating the major elements of the group, the leader, the quality of materials, the environment, and organizational components. It does not provide for evaluation of learning: That is, it does not ask how much participants learned about study skills. There are no items asking for feedback on specific leadership skills, only an overall rating for the leader. If one group objective were to improve leadership skills, the form would need items that specifically relate to leadership skills, such as reflected content and meaning.

Instrumentation

Once you decide on the elements you want to evaluate, you must consider your instrumentation. Some groups lend themselves to standardized tests or rating scales. This is particularly true for social or life skills groups and for some educational groups, such as those that focus on career education. You will find many standardized tests and scales. In reviewing these, you should pay attention to the established validity for the kind of participants in the group, particularly in regard to age, gender, racial/ethnic group, and educational level. Reliability, usability, and cost are other factors in choosing a standardized test or rating scale.

Standardized tests and rating scales are useful when you want to determine or document changes that occur as a result of the group. For example, funding for career education groups may depend on how well learning is achieved in existing groups. Careful evaluation, using valid standardized tests, can give evidence to support continuation or may suggest that other avenues should be explored. Standardized tests and scales also allow you to make comparisons with previous groups.

Most often, however, leaders of psychoeducational groups do not use standardized instruments for evaluation because they are too expensive, they do not meet specific group needs, they are not designed around the group's topic, or the leader lacks the training to use them. If a standardized instrument is desirable and available, and cost is not a concern, a testing consultant may be used.

The majority of psychoeducational groups can get the data they need from carefully constructed instruments tailored to their groups. Designing and constructing such an instrument calls for expertise in the field and a knowledge of qualitative evaluation and of various evaluation techniques. For the best possible evaluation, you should work with a consultant who has this expertise during the planning phase.

Despite these constraints, you can evaluate your group without paying an expert consultant, even if you are not an expert in the field yourself. The evaluation will be limited and the data will not be as extensive, but it can provide valuable information for designing and conducting future groups. The following guidelines are designed to help you develop a group-specific form, even if you are not an expert in evaluation.

Constructing an Instrument

After deciding on which objectives and strategies you want to evaluate, you must choose which and how many areas to evaluate, decide how in-depth the items should be and the maximum number of items for each subarea, select what scale you will use, and decide whether you will ask for open ended comments. The form may also contain items that evaluate participants' interest in additional groups.

Selecting Areas. Table 7.5 lists three primary areas for evaluation: structure, program or content, and leadership. Under each area are several subareas, under which one or more items could be constructed. Altogether there are 21 subareas listed. If only an overall rating is used for each, this produces 21 items. Most participants are more inclined to evaluate the experience when there are a moderate number of items, such as 10 to 15. Therefore, it is useful to select 3 or 4 subareas, write 2 to 3 items about each, and use overall ratings for the remainder.

Use several items instead of one global or overall rating for a subarea allows for better definition of strengths and weaknesses. For example, the subarea "facilities" could contain items such as these:

5 = excellent; 4 = good; 3 = adequate; 2 = fair; 1 = poor

Comfort of seating	5	4	3	2	1
Temperature control	5	4	3	2	1
Free of outside distractions	5	4	3	2	1
Availability, cost, & convenience of parking	5	4	3	2	1
Convenience of access	5	4	3	2	1
Proximity of restrooms, eating spots, telephones, etc.	5	4	3	2	1

TABLE 7.5
Areas for Evaluation

Areas	Topics
Structure	Organization
	Facilities
	Materials
	Media
	Providing for input, interaction
	Scheduling for events, breaks
	Objectives
Program or Content	Mini-lectures
	Games (e.g., icebreakers)
	Exercises
	Handouts
	Meeting of personal needs or objectives
	Discussion
	Directions
Leadership	Keeping to schedule
	Responding to participants
	Interest, warmth, enthusiasm showed
	Able to clarify
	Respect for offering opinions and ideas
	Able to keep sessions focused
	Knowledge and understanding of topic

Item Content. After you have chosen the areas and subareas, the total number of items for the form, and the subareas where attention will be focused, you must decide on the content for items under those subareas. The overriding question to address is this: What is most important to know about this subarea?

Even this short question may produce more topics than can be accommodated. Prioritizing is helpful at this point, with the more important topics receiving separate items and others combined into more global items. For example, assume that the subarea "games" was selected. Some topics would include number of games, timing, objectives, materials, interest, and usefulness. Focusing on the number of games provides data on whether too few or too many were used. It would be helpful for participants to name the games, so that there is not confusion as to what you meant by "games." The item on timing tells you how accurately you anticipated the need for games. Asking for ratings of achievement of the objectives shows if the intended objectives were met. Adequacy of materials used provides information that leads to improvements in the games. The degree of interest participants had in the games is an indicator for further use. This would not be the deciding factor, however, since each group is different. But if you continued to get ratings indicating little or no interest, that game may need to be retired. Using all of these items clarifies the strengths and weaknesses of the game better than a global rating would.

Provision for Rating.   When ratings are used, they are usually in a Likert Scale format. This format uses five labeled categories, each of which has a numerical rating of 1 to 5, with 5 being the most positive. Numerical ratings allow summation and, while they are not entirely psychometrically appropriate, some compilers of the data also compute mean ratings. It is useful to have ratings such as the following:

5 = excellent; 4 = good; 3 = adequate; 2 = fair; 1 = poor.

Provision also can be made for not applicable (NA).

Form Format.   Place the title of the group at the top of the page, the dates of the sessions, and directions. Directions should be specific, brief, and clear. If a rating scale is used, the designations or definitions belong in the directions. It may be helpful to underline directions or put them in **bold** so that they stand out from the rest of the form. Participants will want to know whether the evaluations are anonymous and the use to which they will be put.

Format the items so that the ratings are in rows and columns on the right side of the page. Double-space between items, and provide space between items or at the end for comments. If you are soliciting suggestions for improvements, say so in the directions.

Reduce the font, if necessary, so that the entire form is no more than two pages. One page is preferable, but participants tend not to answer more than two pages.

Chapter 8

EXERCISES AND GAMES

Exercises and games are activities for experiential groups. These terms generally are used interchangeably, but they designate differing purposes in this book. *Exercises* are activities used to promote personal involvement learning, such as communication. *Games* promote other learning, such as time management. Exercises present a range of interrelated factors, while games tend to focus on discrete units.

Exercises and games share some characteristics: Both are brief, simple to implement, use active participation, can be modified easily, and are inexpensive and use few props. The primary differences are the goals, the extent of personal issues involvement, and the need for processing. Exercises usually have broader goals that emphasize more personal issues involvement (for example, increasing self-awareness). They also require more in-depth processing, which focuses on personal learning. Processing is crucial for exercises and is described in the section, "Planning Experiential Group Activities" later in this chapter.

PURPOSES

Exercises and games also share some purposes: as warm-ups and icebreakers, to promote active involvement, to illustrate a point or concept, and as a part of termination. Exercises have a few additional purposes: to promote self-reflection, to increase self-awareness, and to increase self-knowledge and self-understanding.

- Participants in psychoeducational groups usually are strangers to one another. Even when members work together, they are somewhat "strangers" in the group setting. An icebreaker/warm-up gets their attention, allows them to meet some other members, and gets the session started. Even in small groups (i.e., five to eight members), an icebreaker/warm-up facilitates the beginning of the group, reduces tension, and relieves some anxiety. Examples of icebreakers/warm-ups are provided later in this chapter.

- Active involvement supports learning, retention, and motivation. Exercises and games call for observable responses, such as oral, movement, drawing, and writing. These usually are easy to do, enjoyable, and have a discernible point, all of which contributes to motivation. Participants are encouraged by success, and exercises and games provide opportunities for success.

- Exercises and games provide alternative ways of presenting material. Where lectures and media presentations hold attention for a relatively short time (e.g., 15 to 20 minutes), even a short exercise or game can keep participants involved and learning for a considerably longer time. It is not unusual for an exercise or game to consume an hour or more, and the leader has to call time.

- Exercises and games also are useful for termination of the group. Termination is as important as beginning the group. Leaders need to plan for termination and closing. It is important not to just stop. If the group has several sessions, each should be ended constructively, not simply stopped. There are exercises and games to effectively terminate and end groups or sessions. Some examples are presented later in this chapter.

RELATIONSHIP TO THEORY

Newstrom and Scannell (1991) described games as incorporating several classical principles of learning, including repetition, reinforcement, association, and use of the senses. The same can be said of exercises, with the addition of personal meaningfulness.

Repetition increases retention of material or skills. Exercises and games allow for repeating or use of concepts, information, skills, and applications.

Reinforcement also contributes to the likelihood of the learned behavior being repeated. Success and other pleasurable consequences are positive reinforcers. Exercises and games are designed to be easily achieved and to be enjoyable, thereby promoting reinforcement.

Association of new material with previously learned material builds learning and understanding. Exercises and games help make gradual transitions and connections between the old and the new. This process promotes learning in a way that reduces anxieties around learning new material.

Increasing use of the senses contributes to more effective learning as well. Exercises and games provide opportunities for participants to use sight, sound, speech, and touch in learning. Further, exercises and games involve the cognitive, affective, and psychomotor domains of learning, making for a more rounded experience.

Meaningfulness of material promotes interest and retention. Exercises are designed to focus on personal involvement issues, leading to participants' having a personal investment in the presented material, which leads to more retention and motivation.

SIMULATIONS AND ROLE-PLAY

Simulations

Simulations are designed to create a significant part or event applicable to a complex organization. They focus on developing solutions to a problem. Simulations present a range of interrelated factors that impact the individual, the problem, the setting, and the organization. Problems are not presented in isolation but in a *simulated* context.

Simulations are used in a variety of settings to present a wide range of problems. For example, simulations are used in educational settings to teach complex problem-solving skills related to economics; in business to address manufacturing production; in public agencies—such as city, state, or federal governmental agencies—to address issues such as global conflicts or transportation problems. Groups work together to define the problem, understand interrelated and complex restraining forces and supporting factors, collect relevant data, analyze the data, and suggest solutions. The "war games" in the Pentagon are an example of simulation on a global scale.

Simulations are usually long-term, that is, they require more than one session; are complex to set up; are intricate to operate; and require ongoing as well as summative processing. It is possible to design a mini-simulation that focuses on a smaller portion or a significant aspect of the problem. These can be accomplished in a briefer time and are useful for teaching problem-solving skills. Mini-simulations are not as useful for understanding complex problems because they are too narrowly focused and time-bound. There also needs to be a learning period, during which participants learn to function in groups, the process for problem-solving, and sources of data. Complex and interrelated situations are not grasped easily or immediately; they need time to be understood.

Role-Play

Role-play attempts to create complex situations with interrelated factors focused on suggesting solutions to problems. Role-play is focused on the individual and his or her personal issues and can be used to recreate a situation to obtain a better understanding of contributing behaviors and other factors; to practice new skills; to extend present knowledge to logical consequences; and to highlight feelings experienced around a circumstance or situation.

Role-play has participants acting "as if": as if they were someone else; as if they were different in some way (e.g., younger); as if circumstances were different; as a part of a future, unknown circumstance or relationship.

Role-play may be structured or unstructured. In structured role-play, participants follow a prescribed script; in unstructured, they are free to develop their own script as the action unfolds.

Processing for role-play is critical, as both players and observers may experience intense feelings. A group leader needs to attend to all participants in some way, and to allow for expression of aroused feelings after the role-play is finished. Role-play can be used effectively in psychoeducational groups, but leaders should be aware of their potential for deepening and intensifying the experience and feelings.

PLANNING EXPERIENTIAL GROUP ACTIVITIES

Experiential group activities can be effective parts of psychoeducational groups. They complement and enhance cognitive material, provide for more active involvement for participants, are enjoyable, and facilitate the movement of the group. Experiential group activities must be planned, however. This initial step is critical if the activity is to be successful.

Goals

Planning incorporates goals, the participants, and environmental concerns. Specific experiential activities are selected only after goals and objectives have been established. The activities are strategies to help accomplish the goals and objectives, so they should have clear and direct connections to the goals or objectives.

For example, the goal for a group may be to learn time management strategies. An objective would be for each participant to become aware of his or her peak energy time so as to plan the most complex tasks of the day to occur at that time. The experiential activity would be to have each participant recreate on paper the previous day's activities, emotions experienced during the activities, and the degree of difficulty of the activities. Participants could then divide into time period subgroups to discuss possible strategies for capitalizing on their peak energy periods.

Participants

Experiential activities should be selected with the participants' age, maturity, and other readiness factors in mind. Although it generally is possible to use almost any activity with any group after suitable modifications, some activities are most suitable for adults in a particular setting (for example, work). For example, an in-basket exercise would not be appropriate for children who have no knowledge or understanding of how an office functions.

On the other hand, some exercises work for almost any group, such as "Draw a Conflict" (Exercise 8.10). This exercise can be easily adapted for children or adults, for personal or work situations, and for various educational levels. Through experience, you will learn which experiential activities should be restricted to certain participants, and which can be adapted and modified for differing groups.

Physical Facilities

A variety of factors are incorporated under environmental concerns: time, setting, group size, materials needed, and staffing. Structural variables and details have a significant impact on the functioning of the group, learning for participants, and the success and effectiveness of experiential activities.

Time. Time refers to the time available for the group, the session, and the activity. A particular activity may meet all of the previous requirements but consume considerable time to complete. The time used for that activity may be needed to accomplish other group objectives. Some flexibility should be built into the schedule to allow time to complete activities. It is not possible to accurately and precisely plan the exact time needed for any activity. All groups differ, and even when an activity is the same, each group will respond somewhat differently. However, you can approximate the time needed and you should be willing to either move on if it take less time than anticipated or allow enough time to complete the activity.

An important point to remember is that activities should be completed, not stopped or truncated. You can never know for sure if there is some personal involvement issue that has been touched on for participants. These participants should not be left dangling, and they are unlikely to speak up or to ask for guidance.

Environmental Concerns. Physical facilities contribute to the effective functioning of the group. The room should be big enough so that participants do not feel crowded, have adequate temperature controls, and have sufficient comfortable seating. If participants are to participate in small or subgroup activities that involve writing or drawing, tables that seat five to seven or breakout rooms with tables are preferable. It is not desirable to have desks, fixed tables and chairs, or an arrangement that provides barriers to group communication. Moveable seating is useful, particularly if there are to be demonstrations.

Environmental concerns also include attention to privacy, noise control, and interruptions. Safety and trust needs are addressed, in part, when facilities are such that participants will not be heard by outsiders, and outsiders cannot drop in unexpectedly to interrupt. Noise control also helps keep distractions at a minimum.

Group Size. You should choose activities appropriate for the size of your group. An activity that uses a considerable amount of time for processing is more appropriate for a small group, in which each member has ample time for input. An activity that needs your expertise for processing is more appropriate for a small group than a large group.

Psychoeducational groups tend to have large numbers of participants, and activities should reflect the constraints imposed by the number of participants. Activities that provide for breaking the large group into smaller groups, and for which processing does not require the leader, can be effective in enhancing learning. Selecting topics that can be discussed in leaderless groups is another component. Controversial topics should be reserved for smaller groups, where the leader can block inappropriate input, help work through differences, and provide safety. The focus for most psychoeducational groups is on learning, not on working through personal issues or problems.

Materials Needed. All materials needed to complete an activity should be gathered in advance. Participants should not have to share materials. You should have enough of everything so that there are extras.

Materials should be selected carefully. If preprinted forms or questionnaires are used, the font should allow for easy reading. Purchased tests or other materials should have reading levels appropriate for the educational level of participants. Some suggestions follow for selecting materials for drawing-related exercises:

- Provide paper in large enough quantities so that group members can make mistakes. The sheets should be large enough for expression, about 18" by 24". Newsprint is adequate and has the advantage of being less costly than other kinds of paper. Paper should be neutral in color; colored construction paper is not recommended for drawing activities.

The art exercise should be selected for a particular purpose, and the same is true for your choice of media. Most drawing exercises can be accomplished with graphite pencils, charcoal, chalk pastels, oil pastels, felt-tip watercolors, or crayons. Each has specific qualities that contribute to the pleasure derived from doing art.

- Pencils have the advantage of being readily available and come with degrees of soft to hard lead. Soft lead doesn't take much physical pressure to make marks, but it smears easily. Children are very sensitive to "messing up" and may get upset if their drawing is smudged.

- Charcoal is easy to grasp, makes marks easily, can be smudged for shading effects, and can be used as a stick or with fingers to make designs. It is very messy, however, and cleanup materials should be kept at hand.

- Chalk pastels come in colors that are easily transferred to paper. Color can be layered, mixed, or smudged. As with charcoal, cleanup materials are necessary.

- Oil pastels glide easily on paper and have easy applicability, like chalk pastels, but they have the added advantage of being less messy. Colors are brilliant and can be mixed, overlaid, rubbed, or smudged.

- Felt-tip watercolors are available at very little cost in a vast array of colors. They can be secured in either fine line or broad tips, clean up easily, and are easily applied to paper. Some are even scented.

- Crayons are also available in a vast array of colors. They are not messy, but there is some resistance when applied to paper. They do not glide as easily as felt-tips, chalk pastels, and oil pastels. Use crayons if other materials are not available in supplies sufficient for each member to have what he or she needs.

There are other media that can provide a satisfying experience. However, be careful that the emphasis is on the experience—and not on the end product.

Staffing. If you are leading a large psychoeducational group, you will find it helpful to have an assistant, who can help distribute and take up materials, secure additional materials if needed, help answer questions, coordinate breaks, and run media machines. This assistance frees you to concentrate on the group and activities.

Some groups have coleaders. It is essential that co-leaders be familiar with each other's working style. It is easy for conflict to emerge between co-leaders, and conflict affects the functioning of the group, even when it goes unexpressed. Co-leaders have a lot of personal work to do before trying to lead a group together.

If there are assistants involved in addition to the group leader, it is important that pregroup meetings be held. People who are expected to work together need time to understand their roles and functions, expectations, and the goals of the group. They can help set the agenda and work out specific duties. Pregroup meetings facilitate the process of working together and help minimize misunderstandings and conflicts.

EXERCISES AND GAMES

Following are 10 exercises and games that can be used with a variety of age groups. Although they have been categorized (e.g., as icebreakers), most can be adapted for other objectives. Each is presented using the format below.

Title: The title is descriptive of the exercise or game.

Category: The category defines the primary use for the exercise.

Objectives: This is a list of what personal learning or group task the exercise is intended to accomplish—the emphasis or focus for the exercise.

Materials: This is a list of materials needed such as forms, tests, drawing materials, tables, etc.

Time: This is the approximate length of time the exercise will take to complete.

Age/Education: Ages and educational levels of participants for which the exercise is most suited will be listed here.

Number of Participants: Specified here is the maximum number of participants, or a range, with whom the exercise can be managed most effectively.

Preparation: This section describes what needs to be done to prepare to conduct the exercise (e.g., develop examples of products such as seals or collages, reproduce handouts, plan strategies for working with small groups, etc.).

Procedure: This is a description of a suggested way of introducing the activity and organizing participants. Approximate time frames for different parts of the activity also are presented.

Processing: This section provides samples of questions and statements to help focus the activity on the most important learning objectives.

Adaptations: This section notes if the exercise can be adapted for use with other age groups; directions for adaptation are included.

There are several categories for exercises and games. However, this list will present only five: icebreakers, team or group building, communicating verbally, communicating nonverbally, and termination. Other exercises and games are presented throughout the book.

EXERCISE 8.1. BIRTHDAYS

Category: Game; icebreaker

Objectives: To energize the group; to relieve tension and anxiety; to help participants identify similarities among themselves

Materials: None

Time: 10 to 15 minutes, depending on size of group

Age/Education: Almost any age except for very young children, who do not know the sequence for months in the year; all educational levels, except as noted for age levels

Number of Participants: Unlimited

Preparation: None needed

Procedure: The leader tells participants they are to line up in order of the month and day of their birthdays, beginning with January 1. Designate where the line is to begin and tell participants to begin lining up.

Watch the process participants use to order themselves. Notice who takes the lead for a particular month, the number who seem to have birthdays on the same day, and so on.

After the line is complete, ask participants to quickly say their birthday's month and day. Note clustering, gaps, birthdays that occur on major holidays, and so on.

Processing: Repeat some of your observations to the group—how they seemed tentative in getting started, how the lead was assumed. Some questions could be these: What did you feel as you were doing this? Were there any surprises? What impressions do you have of fellow participants after completing the game?

EXERCISE 8.2. FIND SOMEONE WHO ...

Category: Game; icebreaker

Objectives: To energize the group; to introduce participants; to reduce tension

Materials: A copy of Handout 8.2. "Find Someone Who . . . " for each participant; pencils or pens

Time: 15 to 20 minutes

Age/Education: All; revise for children

Number of Participants: 25 to 30

Preparation: Reproduce Handout 8.2, "Find Someone Who . . . "; gather other materials.

Procedure: Tell participants that this is a get acquainted activity designed to help them meet each other and to find out a piece of information about each other. It will require that they move around and talk to each other.

Pass out Handout 8.2 and pencils or pens. Tell participants they are to mill around, find a person who meets the description for each sentence, and write their names in the space provided. Participants may use their own names for one description, where appropriate. They will have _____ minutes to complete Handout 8.2.

Processing: Stop the action after the designated time. Ask for a show of hands for those who were able to fill in all of the blanks. Select five or six items and ask the person who fits the description to stand or raise his or her hand.

Adaptations: Change the items to reflect what is or can be inferred about the participants. For example, for a group of managers, there could be an item about owning a motorcycle or working in a political campaign.

Find Someone Who ...

1. Has a birthday in June:_____

2. Likes math:_____

3. Plays a musical instrument:_____

4. Likes to grow vegetables:_____

5. Draws (pictures, etc.): _____

6. Can sew: _____

7. Likes to cook:_____

8. Has a dog:_____

9. Likes to read for pleasure:_____

10. Watches football on TV:_____

11. Has yellow as a favorite color:_____

12. Is good at sports:_____

13. Likes to dance:_____

14. Can ride a horse:_____

15. Would like to travel to a foreign country:_____

16. Attends movies frequently:_____

17. Looks forward to the year's beginning:

18. Watches situation comedies on TV:_____

19. Listens to classical music:_____

20. Collects things (e.g., buttons): _____

Handout 8.2. Find Someone Who ... . *Permission is granted to photocopy for group use.*

EXERCISE 8.3. GROUP IDENTIFICATION

Category: Exercise; team building

Objectives:To help members get acquainted; to build group identity and cohesion

Materials: Written directions; a sheet of paper 20" by 30" or larger, with a large circle drawn in the center (the circle should take up most of the page); masking tape; set of felt-tip markers in various colors for each group; table or desk and space or rooms for groups; an example of a group seal prepared in advance (see Figure 8.1)

Time: 60 to 90 minutes

Age/Education: All

Number of Participants: 50

Preparation: Reproduce written directions for the exercise, develop an example for a group seal using the same materials as will the participants.

Procedure: Tell members they will meet in small groups throughout the time period of the workshop. As a beginning, they will be divided into small groups to get to know each other, decide on a name for the group, and develop a group seal formed of symbols describing group members. Divide the large group into smaller groups of five to eight members. Give each group its materials and the time allotted to complete the task. Twenty to 30 minutes may be sufficient, although groups may need more time. Be sure to allot sufficient time for processing. At the end of the allotted time period, check with groups and determine if more time is needed. If so, give groups an additional 10 to 15 minutes. Remind groups to choose a name.

Processing: Reassemble small groups into one large group. Post seals where they can be easily seen. Have a member from each group describe the group's seal and the meaning for the group's name. Questions can focus on feelings about the group as presented through the names and seals. No in-depth interpretation or analyses of symbols should be allowed.

Figure 8.1. Example of a group seal.

EXERCISE 8.4. PREVIEW

Category: Game; communicating verbally

Objectives: To help members focus on learning tasks; to make members aware of cognitive material; to prepare members to learn

Materials: 5" by 8" cards; paper and pencil or pen for the recorder of each group; terms or concepts preprinted on newsprint or transparency

Time: 20 to 30 minutes

Age/Education: Reading ability at or above fourth-grade level

Number of Participants: Unlimited

Preparation: Prior to the session, you should prepare a card for each participant that has a list of major terms and concepts relating to the topic and material that is the focus for the group. Include terms that will be defined and illustrated in presentations. Younger participants should have shorter lists.

Procedure: Tell members they will be divided into smaller groups to briefly discuss their understandings of the terms and concepts. Each group will select a recorder, who will report to the larger group. Members are not expected to know all of the terms and concepts. Give the groups the time frame for the discussion (e.g., 20 minutes).

Divide the large group into smaller groups and tell where each is to meet (e.g., a corner of room). Give a group member the paper and pencil to be given to the recorder. After groups go to their designated spaces, you should visit each group to answer any questions, to reassure that they are not expected to know all of the material, and to remind them of the time.

Processing: After the large group reassembles, ask the recorder for each group to report on two or three of the terms and concepts. After each set, ask if any group had different meanings from the one reported. After all groups have reported, ask if there are some terms and concepts that were unfamiliar to every group. This activity provides a lead-in to a mini-lecture or presentation.

EXERCISE 8.5. COLLABORATIVE DRAWING

Category: Exercise; communicating nonverbally

Objectives: To introduce the concept of working together cooperatively; to demonstrate nonverbal ways of communicating; to highlight differing ways of approaching a task

Materials: Newsprint 20" by 30" or larger; a set of felt-tip markers or crayons for each pair of participants; masking tape; tables where pairs can work undisturbed

Time: 30 to 90 minutes

Age/Education: All

Number of Participants: 5 to 50

Preparation: Gather materials and organize room for group drawing.

Procedure: Pass out the paper and markers. Introduce the exercise by telling participants they will pair off and collaborate on a drawing without talking or verbally communicating. Have participants pair up and go to the space where they will do the drawing.

Each person selects one color. Only this color will be used by the person for the drawing. Without talking or writing, the pairs begin to draw a picture. They can take turns or work at the same time. The can begin in any way they like. The time allotted for the task is _____ minutes. After drawing, each person is to give it a title. While the participants are working, you should watch each group: how they get started, who begins, if they work on separate sides of the paper, if they elaborate on each other's drawings. Watch for laughter, signs of frustration or resistance, and so on.

Processing: Call time and collect the drawings. If they have not been titled, ask partners to title them. Post the drawings where they are visible to the entire group. Ask participants to walk around and look at all of the drawings.

After a short time, ask questions such as: What was it like to have to work without talking? What was difficult? What was easy? You can report some of the behaviors you observed during the activity.

EXERCISE 8.6. THE COLOR WHEEL

Category: Game or exercise

Objectives: *Game*—To help members get to know each other; to have fun; to relieve tension

Exercise—To help members identify intensities of feelings; to focus on feelings; to learn additional adjectives for expressing feelings

Materials: Sets of paint chips in 10 to 15 different colors, with enough sets so that each group has a complete set, or use strips of construction paper; list of colors for each participant—colors used and gradations of them should be mounted on a large piece of poster board in a color wheel; pencils; newsprint; masking tape

Time: 30 to 60 minutes

Age/Education: All

Number of Participants: Unlimited

Preparation: Prepare color wheel on poster board using the same materials as participants will use; reproduce list of available colors, enough for each participant to have a list; gather other materials.

Procedure: Tell participants they will be divided into groups to discuss their associations of feelings with colors. Each group is to come to a consensus on which color is associated with a particular feeling: for example, red associated with love. Give a time frame for the task.

Pass out lists of colors and pencils. Divide the large group into small groups and tell groups where they are to meet. Give each group a board with the colors mounted on it, and ask them to designate a recorder.

Processing: When the large group reassembles, ask each group to report on the associations for each color. Record these on newsprint. Post the newsprint so that the entire group can see it.

Point out similarities and differences in associations. The prepared wheel can then be discussed and differences in intensity of feelings emphasized: for example, irritation, annoyance, anger, rage.

EXERCISE 8.7. ALL ABOUT ME

Category: Game or exercise

Objectives: *Game*—To get acquainted; to have fun

Exercise—Self-disclosure

Materials: 5" by 8" cards; plastic sandwich bags; cut-out pictures; glue sticks; felt-tip markers; scissors; a model mini-collage; tables

Time: 30 to 90 minutes

Age/Education: All

Number of Participants: Used as a game, an unlimited number of participants; used as an exercise, a maximum of 30 participants

Preparation: Prior to the group, cut out pictures and put a variety in each sandwich bag. Prepare enough bags so that each participant will have one. Sources for pictures are catalogs and magazines. If the activity is to be done with children, cut the pictures out carefully so that no further cutting is needed. Adolescents and adults can finish trimming.

Make one or more examples of a mini-collage. These should reflect a theme such as "my values," "who am I," "my favorite things or pastimes," or "my dreams or wishes for the future." If used as a game, make the theme superficial. Exercises require more personal involvement and self-disclosure. Use this activity as an exercise only when a deeper experience is needed to accomplish the group goal, such as anger management.

Procedure: Introduce the exercise by telling participants the activity is to help them introduce themselves in a different way. Show the examples and explain that they will be given the materials to make a mini-collage about themselves around the theme you have chosen. Give them the time frame, usually 15 to 30 minutes. Break the large group into small groups of five to seven members and tell them where they are to meet. Have all meeting spaces in the same room so you can move between groups. Small groups meet around tables to work. If possible, have cards, sandwich bags of pictures, glue sticks, and other materials already placed on the tables. Participants are allowed to talk and to exchange pictures.

After the allotted time, stop the construction and ask participants to share their mini-collages in their small groups. Tell them how much time will be available for this step.

Processing: *Game*—Focus on feelings experienced while constructing the mini-collage, adequacy of pictures, and what it was like to get to know someone this way.

Exercise—Ask the same questions as for the game, but try to get each participant to respond to each question. Explore expressions of dislike or negativity as well as those that are positive by asking the participant to explain further. Asking, "What was it about _____ that produced this feeling?" is one way to explore.

EXERCISE 8.8. ROUND ROBIN DRAWING

Category: Game or exercise

Objectives: *Game*—To have fun; to get acquainted

Exercise—To build relationships in a small group; termination

Materials: Large (20" by 30" or larger) sheets of newsprint for each participant; set of felt-tip markers, oil pastels, or crayons for each group; masking tape; tables

Time: 15 minutes per small group (four groups per hour)

Age/Education: All

Number of Participants: 35 to 40

Preparation: Gather materials and organize the room.

Procedure: Introduce the activity by telling participants the objective, such as having fun or as a part of termination. If participants have been working in small groups, assign each group to a portion of the room around a group of prearranged tables. If they have not been working in small groups, break the large group into smaller groups of five to seven members. Either pass out paper and markers to each group or have them ready at the assigned tables.

Instruct participants to take a sheet of paper and one marker. Each member in a group should have a different color. Paper is placed flat on the table, and members instructed to stand. Ask participants to look at their paper and either to think about their group or to anticipate the group experience. Tell them you will give a signal and they are to make a mark on their paper—any mark, anywhere. At the next signal, they are to move one place to the right, look at that sheet of paper with its mark, and add to it with their marker, and so on. They are to use the same marker throughout the exercise. Keep moving participants around until they get back to their original sheets. Tell them to finish their pictures and give them a title. Give signals every 10 to 15 seconds; children may need a little longer.

After the drawings are completed, have each group post their drawings where the group can see it and sit down with their group.

Processing: Processing involves small groups responding in the context of the larger group. If the activity is used as a game, confine questions to these: What do you think of your drawing as it turned out? How did you feel during the activity? Allow time for participants to roam around and view other groups' drawings.

If used as an exercise, begin with the questions used in the game. Add questions that focus more on feelings about the topic, that is, the group. Ask about the association of the title each group gave the drawings, if there were any surprises, and if they like how their drawings turned out. Also allow some time for viewing by all participants.

EXERCISE 8.9. I LEARNED ... , I REMEMBERED ...

Category: Game; termination

Objectives: To terminate; to focus learning

Materials: 5" by 8" cards; pens or pencils

Time: 45 to 60 minutes

Age/Education: Fifth grade and above

Number of Participants: Unlimited

Preparation: Gather materials and develop an example for each category such as that listed below in "Procedure."

Procedure: Introduce the game as part of termination of the group. Summarize all of the activities that have taken place. Give each participant a card and ask members to list two to five points they learned or remembered or that were meaningful for them in some way. Give an example of what could be listed:

● **Learned**: To prioritize daily activities and work on most important ones first.

● **Remembered**: It's easier to ask for cooperation than to demand it, and people respond more positively to a request.

● **Meaningful**: How I feel about something makes a big difference in my responses, and I am not always conscious of how I feel.

Processing: If participants have worked in small groups, have them discuss their points in those groups. If not, divide them into small groups for the discussion. Tell them the time frame for the discussion.

After the small group discussion, have each group report a sample of the points, with particular emphasis on similarities.

EXERCISE 8.10. DRAW A CONFLICT

Category: Exercise

Objectives: To increase awareness of personal contributions to conflicts; to suggest alternative behaviors in conflicts

Materials: Drawing materials appropriate for the age group—for example, crayons for elementary school children; large sheets of newsprint

Time: 30 minutes to 2 hours

Age/Education: All

Number of Participants: Small groups (can be used with 30 to 35)

Preparation: Gather materials

Procedure: Tell participants to think of a conflict they had with another person. It can be a current one, one of long-standing, or one that was resolved. It is best if the conflict is one that is of importance for them.

After they have identified the conflict, instruct the participants to select a scene that illustrates for them the essence of the conflict and to draw it. Allow enough time for participants to reflect and to draw.

Processing: Participants can share their drawings in small groups, or if the group has less than 10 members, they can share with the entire group. They are instructed not to make value judgements about someone's conflict but can ask clarifying questions. After the sharing period, ask each small group to select one conflict to role-play.

The role-play is directed by the person with the conflict; however, this person does not play any of the roles. He/she describes the situation and the players so that other group members can play the roles.

One at a time, the conflicts are role-played before the large group. After each role-play, debrief the participants and director by asking how accurate the portrayal of the conflict was and how each person feels. You also can ask if the director can see other ways to handle the conflict and solicit suggestions from the other players. It is important to have some debriefing of role-players and directors.

Chapter 9

EDUCATIONAL GROUPS: DEFINITIONS AND DESCRIPTIONS

Psychoeducational groups whose primary focus is teaching cognitive re-lated material are classified as *educational groups*. Some examples of these are discussion, study skills, career education, alcohol and drug education, and par-ent education groups. In one sense, these groups are classes. They differ from classes in that the goals and objectives are more limited, the time frame is more flexible, no tests or other evaluations of learning are expected, and participants usually are freer to exit.

Educational groups are some of the most structured of the groups discussed in this book, in the sense that the goals and objectives are predetermined and the materials and strategies are preselected by the leader. Participants have little or no input into the agenda, although the leader may decide on adjustments to meet participants' needs. Further, these groups are seldom limited to one ses-sion. Each session should be self-contained, however, so participants can take increased or new knowledge with them. Even parent education groups address a specific topic at each meeting. Having self-contained topics means it is not necessary to know one topic before learning another. The topics are not hierar-chical, but they may be sequential for other reasons, such as increasing sensi-tivity.

Educational groups may have many members, but most are moderate in size to provide opportunities for discussion. Although a large group can be broken down into smaller groups, each needs a facilitator to guide and direct the discussion and to keep it on topic. Groups designed for children, adolescents, and adults have somewhat differing structures. A discussion and sample group materials are presented for each in this chapter.

LEADER SKILLS

The most important skills in leading an educational group are organizing, presenting, linking, blocking, and summarizing. Other skills have a role, as well, but are not as critical as these.

Organizing the group includes determining goals and objectives, selecting strategies, gathering materials, and attending to environmental concerns, such as adequate space. The success of a group depends on the leader's preparation.

Presenting refers to both planning and execution: that is, deciding how to present the material and then carrying it out. Before the group begins, the leader must decide whether to use media, games, exercises, lectures, or a combination of methods. The choices of presentation techniques can make a significant difference in group outcomes.

The leader's interest, enthusiasm, and excitement also play a part in presentation. Getting participants interested leads to more active involvement, which in turn leads to more learning. Effective communication skills—skills such as active listening and responding, clarifying, and summarizing—also facilitate active participation and promote personalized learning. The type of educational focus determines the extent and level of group leadership skills needed.

Linking facilitates learning and promotes universality. Links to previous knowledge and experiences help participants understand meanings and applications for new material.

Blocking is an important skill in educational groups so that storytelling does not consume time needed for learning new material or practicing new skills. Blocking also is used to prevent participants from making comments about each other that are evaluative or judgmental.

Summarizing helps participants review what was learned and tie together pieces of information. Summaries after a presentation, activity, or exercise focus learning and emphasize major points. Summaries at the end of a group highlight the group's accomplishment of goals and objectives.

PSYCHOEDUCATIONAL GROUPS FOR CHILDREN

It is possible to conduct psychoeducational groups for very young children, but this discussion will focus on groups for those ages 7 to 12. Psychoeducational groups are sponsored and conducted in a variety of settings, such as schools, churches, and organizations such as the scouts, boys' and girls' clubs, and the YWCA and YMCA. Groups can be held in one session or in several sessions over a longer period. It is not advisable to hold an extensive one-day session for children.

Basic Considerations

Group Composition. Psychoeducational groups for children will be more effective if participants are in the same age/grade group or within one or two years of each other. The younger the participants, the more homogenous group needs to be in terms of age and grade level. It may be more effective, in some cases, for older children to be in gender-specific groups—that is, all boys or all girls.

Group Size. Two good guides for determining the optimum group size for children are the ages of proposed participants and the number of helpers available in addition to the leader. The younger the proposed participants, the more assistance the leader needs, particularly in view of time constraints. It is advisable to have a helper when the group size is over 10, and to estimate one helper for each set of 10 to 15 participants; that is, you would have two helpers for 30 participants.

Length/Duration/Number of Sessions. Again, the best guide for determining the length, duration, or number of sessions is the age of the participants. Actual working time—not time spent passing out materials or dividing into groups—should be allotted according to the estimated attention span of participants. This is where it is useful to seek guidance from teachers, troop leaders, or other adults who work with the expected participants. Estimate approximately 20 minutes working time for children ages 7 to 9, and 30 to 40 minutes for older children. Group management becomes the primary focus instead of the psychoeducational topic when children's attention span has been exceeded.

If there is to be more than one session around a particular topic, the number and duration of the sessions should be specified in advance. For example, there could be six 30-minute sessions held once a week over six weeks. Planning for each session should be done in advance.

Setting Goals and Objectives.   Develop realistic goals and objectives. Participants' time and attention will be limited, and what can be accomplished in the group will be limited. It is less frustrating to have a few goals and objectives that are met than to have many goals and objectives, few of which are met.

It also may be helpful to include the participants in setting goals and objectives. Getting their input promotes involvement and commitment, both of which enhance group participation. Even if you do not get anything different from what is already planned, simply asking for their input helps promote participants' feelings of being involved.

When conducting psychoeducational groups for children, you should limit goals and objectives to one or to a major few. For example, a series of six sessions around career education may have the overall goal of identifying personal interest related to careers. Objectives for each session would be focused around one of Holland's (1973) interest areas. It then becomes easier to select appropriate activities and strategies.

Too often, group leaders have too many goals and objectives—feeling, for example, that they must address self-confidence, self-esteem, self-awareness, and so on. These topics are too complex and involved to be primary goals and objectives. While some part of them may be addressed or developed through the group, it would be limited and indirect. These can be secondary goals and objectives, but not the main emphases for the group.

Environmental Concerns.   The major environmental concerns are adequate space, appropriate furniture, and freedom from intrusion. You should provide enough room for participants to be comfortably seated without being too close to one another. Children tend to push, shove, and kick at one another when they are too close together, particularly when they do not have enough room to move around in their seats.

Most psychoeducational groups for children use exercises, games, and other active processes. Appropriate furniture contributes to the success of the group. Most desirable are tables around which five to seven participants can sit, and chairs in which participants can sit comfortably with their feet resting on the floor and not dangling. If there are multiple tables, there should be sufficient space between them for the leader and helpers to move between them and to allow those at one table to talk to each other without overdue intrusion of noise from another table.

Freedom from intrusion also refers to intrusive noises and people. Outside noises and interruptions are disruptive to the group process and do not promote feelings of safety. While confidentiality is not so much a primary concern as in a counseling group, participants feel safer if they know they will not be overheard or interrupted.

Following is a sample group exercise designed for children. It can be used for older groups with little or no modification. More time can be allowed for subsequent discussion with older participants. It can be self-contained or used as part of a several-session group.

EXERCISE 9.1. WHO AM I? A COLLAGE EXERCISE

Objective: To help participants identify important aspects of self that lead to clarification of interests related to careers

Materials: 5" by 8" cards; glue sticks; felt-tip markers; cut-out pictures; pencils; newsprint; masking tape

Time: One 30- to 40-minute session

Age/Education: 8- and 9-year-olds

Number of Participants: Unlimited

Preparation: Before the group begins, the leader and helpers cut pictures from magazines and catalogs that symbolize or depict the following: colors, hobbies, sports, workers, animals, gardens, trees, flowers, cars, trucks, vans, space ships, airplanes, computers and software, music, books, and other things that children like to do or may have an interest in. There should be enough pictures for each participant to have a variety from which to choose. Place a variety of pictures in a box for each table. It is better to have too many pictures than too few.

Also prepare on newsprint lists of interests and characteristics associated with each category for Holland's (1973) typology. Other career development theories that use interests (such Kuder's, 1963, 1987)

can be used. These will be posted *after* participants have finished their collages.

The leader should prepare two to three examples of a collage, each containing pictures or symbols for the following characteristics: my favorite activity, best school subject, kind of work I think I would like, how I am creative, favorite color, favorite hobby or sport, what I like learning about, something I do really well, and something I do not like to do.

On one side of each 5" by 8" card list the same characteristics that comprise the collage, each on a separate line.

Procedure: Introduce the exercise by pointing out that knowing who you are, what you like, and what you dislike helps you sort through the many available careers to find out which you like best. While knowing what you like to do is only one part of selecting a career, it is an important part.

Pass out cards to participants, put boxes of pictures, glue sticks, pencils, and felt-tip markers on each table.

After all items have been read, show the prepared collages and point out the pictures used for each item. Instruct participants to make their own collages on the other side of their cards using the pictures in the box and felt-tip markers for drawing. If they do not have the specific picture they want, they can use something that is a symbol for it or draw it. Allow 10 minutes for them to complete the collage.

Allow 5 to 10 minutes for participants to share their collages with others at their table. While they are doing so, post the newsprint with the characteristics on the wall.

After each member has had an opportunity to share in the small group, focus their attention on the posted characteristics and instruct participants to find the one that is most like them. They do not have to have each characteristic, but most of what they wrote about themselves should fit into the category. You can help participants understand the similarities. Participants can write the name of the category on their cards for future reference.

Processing: End the exercise by asking for responses. What did they like? Dislike? What was easy to do? Hard to do? Did they learn anything about themselves or about others in their group?

PSYCHOEDUCATIONAL GROUPS FOR ADOLESCENTS

Basic Considerations

Most adolescents have sufficient attention spans to benefit from an extended psychoeducational group. A two- to three-hour group provides more time to cover a topic in-depth but is not usually so long as to produce boredom. A day-long group may be too long for younger adolescents, but a well-planned one may be effective for older ones. If the group is to be longer than 50 to 60 minutes, you should have a variety of activities that require active participation and provide for small group interaction. It is also advisable to have a helper for more than 10 participants.

Group Composition. Restrict the range of ages and grade levels to no more than two years or grades. For example, it would not be productive to have 13- and 17-year-olds in the same group. For some topics, such as health education, it may be advisable to have same-gender groups to reduce embarrassment and promote interaction on sensitive topics.

There may be little or no opportunity for you to screen group members, but simply knowing who has difficulty paying attention, who is inclined to be disruptive or aggressive, and who is shy can help in your planning. Consult with teachers, counselors, and others who work or interact frequently with proposed participants.

Group Size. You should plan to divide larger groups into small ones of five to seven members, with a helper for every two to three small groups. The helper can move between the groups to distribute materials, to answer questions, and to manage behavior. The helper's presence is often enough to reduce disruptive behavior and to keep arguments from escalating. Organizing the group in this way enables you to present to larger groups.

Length/Duration/Number of Sessions. Adolescents can tolerate more in-depth sessions than children can. They also remember more over time, even with intervening events. For these reasons, psychoeducational groups for adolescents can be longer, greater in number, and held over a longer time period. Sometimes the setting—such as school, church, or club—will dictate the length, duration, and number of sessions. The topic also plays a part, as some topics require more sessions than others. For example, career education covers more extensive material and requires more sessions than test-taking skills.

Setting Goals and Objectives.   As with children, it is useful to set limited, realistic goals and objectives for adolescent psychoeducational groups. There may be a need for extensive information on the part of the participants, but there also is a limit to how much they can absorb and learn. Some topics may have an extensive emotional component that also limits how much can be taken in. Give participants as much information as they can use, but not so much that they tune it out.

It is useful to elicit participants' input into the goal and objectives of the group. Whenever possible, incorporate their suggestions and point out how you have done so. Share your developed goal and objectives and ask if these seem to meet their expectations and needs. Participants are likely to be more active when they have some personal interest.

Environmental Concerns.   The same concerns listed for groups with children (for adequate space, furniture, and freedom from intrusion) apply to adolescent groups. Physically, adolescents are much larger, and many (especially younger ones) have not adjusted to their bodies. For example, they may not realize that being five inches taller means they take up more space. Adequate space is important to provide comfort and sufficient personal space.

Tables and chairs should be adequate for all planned activities. When attached seats and desks must be used, they should be formed into a circle for the small groups.

Freedom from intrusion is important for adolescent groups. This is not so much to preserve confidentiality; adolescents typically do not want adults to hear what they are saying. While they do not become as easily distracted, interruptions can be distracting enough to get them off the subject, making it difficult to maintain the group mood.

Following is a sample program with an educational emphasis for adolescents. This group can be used as an extended presentation or for short sessions over time. The materials include three exercises, two handouts, an example of topics and strategies, and a sample schedule for a one-day presentation.

PROGRAM 9.1. STUDY SKILLS GROUP FOR ADOLESCENTS

Objectives: To identify needed time management activities that will increase study skills; to increase awareness of time available for study and need for scheduling; to review or learn effective study skills habits; to identify personal study habits

Materials: Copies of Handouts 9.2. 9.3, 9.4A, and 9.4B for each participant; name tags; pens or pencils; tables where groups of five can work and hold discussions

Time: 6 to 12 hours (a one-day workshop or a series of one-hour sessions)

Age/Education: Adolescents

Number of Participants: Upper limits of 5 to 10 members if used as a group over time; 30 to 35 members if used as a workshop

Preparation: Review literature on study skills training and its effectiveness for the target group; survey or conduct interviews to determine the needs of participants; and develop a schedule for presentation.

Example of Topics and Strategies

Topics	Strategy
Survey of study habits and skills	Exercise & Handout 9.2
Effective study skills	Exercise & Handout 9.3
Increasing academic effectiveness	Exercise 9.4 & Handout 9.4A
Tools for academic achievement	Handout 9.4B
Suggested additional mini-lectures (not included)	
Note taking	
Test-taking skills	
Reading improvement	
Memory systems	

Sample Schedule for a One-Day Session

Topic	Activity
Introductions	Get acquainted icebreaker (not included)
Overview	Review goal, objectives and proposed schedule including breaks. Solicit input and additional objectives.
My Study Habits	Exercise 9.2. Survey of Study Habits and Skills
Results of Survey	Discussion
Break	
Tips for Better Study Skills	Exercise 9.3. Effective Study Skills (& Handout 9.3)
Personal Barriers	Brainstorm personal barriers to effective study stills and post on newsprint. Discuss.
Break or Lunch	
Study Skills Time Management	Exercise 9.4. Increasing Academic Effectiveness, with discussion (& Handout 9.4A)
Break	
Tools for Academic Achievement	Handout 9.4B. Tools for Academic Achievement
Termination	Closing exercise (not included)

EXERCISE 9.2. SURVEY OF STUDY HABITS AND SKILLS

Objectives: To identify skills that need to be developed or increased; to identify habits that need to be decreased or eliminated

Materials: Handout 9.2; pencils; large newsprint; masking tape

Time: 60 to 90 minutes

Age/Education: 5th grade reading level and above

Number of Participants: 35

Preparation: Gather materials and organize room.

Procedure: Distribute Handout 9.2 and pencils. Tell participants that the first step in understanding their study habits and skills is identifying current behaviors. Ask them to fill out Handout 9.2 and add their ratings in each category. While they do this, post five sheets of paper with a category printed at the top of each: Environmental Concerns, Time Management, Organizing, Controlling, and Communication.

When participants have completed scoring, divide them into small groups of four to six members. Ask groups to discuss the high and low categories and to keep a list of the five items receiving the highest scores and the five receiving the lowest scores. Allow them 10 to 15 minutes to complete this.

Ask each group in turn to report on the five highest rated items and write the item number on the appropriate category sheet of newsprint. When an item is selected more than once, put a tally mark beside it. Draw a line across each sheet and have groups report the lowest rated number. Repeat the recording and tally.

Processing: Lead a discussion on the habits and skills most frequently used. Focus on barriers or constraints that prevent participants from using certain habits and skills. Finally, have participants finish these statements by selecting one of the skills or habits:

I need to increase ...
I need to decrease ...

Survey of Study Habits and Skills

Directions: Reflect on your usual study behavior and respond to the items using the scale below.

5 = Almost always, always; 4 = Usually; 3 = Sometimes; 2 = Seldom;
1 = Almost never, never

After you complete all the items, add your scores for each section and record them in the blanks.

Environmental Concerns

1. I study in the same place (e.g., bedroom, library) each day.   5   4   3   2   1

2. The place I study is quiet.   5   4   3   2   1

3. I am free from interruptions when I study.   5   4   3   2   1

4. I play background music or the television when I study.   1   2   3   4   5

   Total: _____

Time Management

5. I schedule or arrange time for study each day.   5   4   3   2   1

6. I read class notes shortly after class or before the next class meets.   5   4   3   2   1

7. I study all night before a test.   1   2   3   4   5

8. I read assigned chapters before class.   5   4   3   2   1

9. I keep a calendar of assignments and tests.   5   4   3   2   1

10. I do all assigned homework or more.   5   4   3   2   1

    Total: _____

Organizing

11. I take notes in most classes each day.   5   4   3   2   1

12. I read class handouts, syllabi, etc.   5   4   3   2   1

13. I review tests on file in the library when available.   5   4   3   2   1

14. I attend review sessions.   5   4   3   2   1

15. I use different methods of study for different classes.   5   4   3   2   1

16. I belong to a study group for difficult or demanding courses.   5   4   3   2   1

    Total: _____

Controlling

17. I underline or highlight significant
    material in the textbook.   5   4   3   2   1

18. I outline chapters in textbooks and read
    the outlines.   5   4   3   2   1

19. I make a list or flash cards of vocabulary
    used in the course.   5   4   3   2   1

20. I memorize some content, such as formulas,
    vocabulary, and sequential steps.   5   4   3   2   1

   Total: ___

Communication

21. I meet with the instructor to clarify or
    explain material.   5   4   3   2   1

22. I get help from a tutor.   5   4   3   2   1

23. I ask the instructor or a class member
    for notes when I am absent from class.   5   4   3   2   1

   Total: ___

Scoring
Write your scores in the designated spaces.

Environmental Concerns: ___
(Scores of 12 or below indicate a need for attention.)

Time Management: ___
(Scores of 18 or below indicate trouble with effective time use.)

Organizing: ___
(Scores of 18 or below suggest that basic skills or behaviors need attention.)

Controlling: ___
(Scores of 12 or below indicate that basic skills or behaviors are not used in an
efficient way.)

Communication: ___
(Scores of 9 or below indicate ineffective use of resources.)

I need to increase: _____

I need to decrease: _____

Handout 9.2. Survey of Study Habits and Skills. *Permission is granted to
photocopy for group use.*

EXERCISE 9.3. EFFECTIVE STUDY SKILLS

Objectives: To increase awareness of effective study skills habits and techniques; to increase awareness of ineffective study habits and techniques

Materials: Paper, pencils, newsprint, masking tape

Time: 60 to 90 minutes

Age/Education: 5th grade reading level and above

Number of Participants: 35

Preparation: Gather materials; reproduce Handout 9.3.

Procedure: Prior to distributing Handout 9.3, have the group generate a list of ideas and the study practices they have found effective. It may be helpful to write these on posted newsprint or a chalkboard.

Processing: After the list is generated, distribute Handout 9.3. Effective Study Skills, and briefly discuss each item, giving the advantages of each and suggesting how it can be accomplished. The following can be used as a guide. It may be helpful to have examples of two or three different calendars.

Skill	Advantage(s)	Tool/Strategy
1. Calendar of assignments	Not rushed to complete Submitted on time	Calendar, assignment book
2. Different methods of study	Give more time to more complex courses	Rate, practice, work problems
3. Schedule study time	Breaks it into small manageable units; not as overwhelming	Calendar, half-hour blocks
4. Quiet place	Free from distraction, better concentration	List of quiet places
5. Read handouts, etc.	Understand expectations, gather information	Read immediately, review periodically
6. Read class notes	Fix information in minds, reveal gaps in information	Read immediately, review
7. Read assignments	Prepared for class, can focus on expanding	Read prior to class
8. Take notes or record lectures	Have a record of material, can study for test	Tape recorder, notebook
9. Underline material	Easier to review main points	Highlighter
10. Outline material	Quicker review of main points, definitions, etc.	
11. Vocabulary list	Learn words and concepts for subject	Flash cards, memorization
12. Memorize content	Easier to recall	Rote, practice
13. Homework	Practice, reveal gaps and need for clarification	
14. Attend review sessions	Can get suggestion for test material or focus	
15. Tutors	One-to-one instruction	
16. Study groups	Have demonstrated usefulness; support	Recruit two or three to study with regularly
17. Meet with instructor	Clarify, material, shows interest	Schedule an appointment
18. Review old tests on file	Understand test focus, kind of items, etc.	Ask for old tests or where available

Effective Study Skills

1. Keep a calendar of assignments and tests.

2. Use different methods of study for different classes.

3. Schedule a time for study every day.

4. Have a quiet place for study that is free from distractions and interruptions.

5. Read class handouts, syllabi, and so on.

6. Read class notes immediately after class or before the next class period.

7. Read assigned chapters or other material before class.

8. Take notes in class or record lectures.

9. Underline or highlight significant material in text.

10. Outline chapters and read outline.

11. Compile lists of vocabulary for courses.

12. Memorize content such as formulas.

13. Do *all* assigned homework.

14. Attend review sessions.

15. Seek help from a tutor.

16. Study with a group of students in the class.

17. Meet with the instructor to clarify class material.

18. Review tests on file in the library.

Handout 9.3. Effective Study Skills. *Permission is granted to photocopy for group use.*

EXERCISE 9.4. INCREASING ACADEMIC EFFECTIVENESS

Objectives: To develop awareness of current time use and what changes can be made to increase academic effectiveness; to develop an action plan for study

Materials: Pencils, copies of Handouts 9.4A and 9.4B.

Time: 60 to 90 minutes

Age/Education: 5th grade reading level and above

Number of Participants: 35

Preparation: Gather materials and reproduce Handouts 9.4A and 9.4B.

Procedure: Distribute Handout 9.4A and pencils. Tell participants you will guide them through the exercise. Ask that they move with you in working on items and ask questions. If they do not complete an item in the allotted time, they can return and complete it later.

Describe items 1 through 7, allowing enough time for participants to briefly reflect and write a response. Watch participants to get a sense of when most are ready to move to the next item.

When items 1 through 7 are completed, divide participants into groups of two or three to share their responses. Allow a brief period for sharing, then focus a discussion on what emerged for each item. Have members volunteer what they wrote, but do not judge or evaluate the responses.

The final part (items 8 through 11) is the action plan. Follow the same process used for items 1 through 7.

Distribute Handout 9.4B for participants to read.

Processing: After participants have completed the task in Handout 9.4A, ask for volunteers to share their academic goal and what steps they can take to reach their goal (items 8 through 11).

Increasing Academic Effectiveness

Study Skills Time Management

1. List all classes and their time periods during the week (e.g., English 9 to 10 A.M. Monday through Friday). Total the number of hours for each, and overall

Class	Time	Days	Total hours for class

Total hours: _____

2. Rate the degree of difficulty you experience for each class using the following scale: 5 = extremely difficult; 4 = very difficult; 3 = difficult; 2 = not usually difficult; 1 = easy.

Class	Difficulty Rating

3. List other responsibilities (e.g., work), commitments (e.g., church), and meetings (e.g., club) you had during the previous week, and an estimate of the amount of time each took. Include travel time if it applies.

Event	Time Consumed

Total Estimated Time Consumed: _____

4. Estimate the amount of time you used for each of the following study-related activities during the previous week:

Activity	Time
Planning (e.g., writing a to-do list)	_____
Scheduling (e.g., writing specific times for events)	_____
Organizing (e.g., review, reading)	_____
Controlling (e.g., outlining, memorizing)	_____
Communication (e.g., clarification of class material)	_____
Total:	_____

5. Estimate the amount of time used the previous week for each of the following:

Sleeping	_____
Eating (include meal preparation time	_____
Grooming (e.g., dressing for the day)	_____
Play, socializing, sports	_____
Talking on the telephone	_____
Watching TV or a video, or listening to music	_____
Household chores (e.g., laundry)	_____
Total:	_____

6. Fill in the blanks with the sums for items 1, 3, 4, and 5, and sum

1. Class time	_____	hours
3. Other responsibilities	_____	hours
4. Activities related to study time	_____	hours
5. Other activities	_____	hours
Total:	_____	

7. Estimate the number of study hours for the previous week:

a. Subtract the total in item 67 from 168
(the number of hours in a seven-day period: _____

This number is the number of hours you have available for study.

b. Compare the estimated number of study hours to the number of hours available for study. It's likely that there are many more hours available than are being used.

c. Go back to item 2 and estimate the time spent in study for each of the classes. Determine if the most difficult classes also consume most of the study time. If there are discrepancies, list the classes that are most difficult but are *not* the ones using the most study time.

Continued on next page

List all classes that do not have two hours of study time for each hour of class time. These are the first priority.

d. Review your estimates for items 3 and 5. List any activities that could be reduced, streamlined, or eliminated:

e. Review your estimates for item 4. List all activities that need more time or attention:

Procedure: Numbers 8 through 11 will be completed later.

8. My academic goal for the semester is:_____

_____

9. I need to increase study time for the following classes (list):_____

_____

10. I need to decrease time spent on the following activities:_____

_____

11. Following are some steps I can take to reach my goal:_____

_____

_____

_____

Handout 9.4A. Increasing Academic Effectiveness. *Permission is granted to photocopy for group use.*

Tools for Academic Achievement

- Set objectives and priorities for class work, and work on them daily.

- Plan the most important task.

- Schedule time for study (daily is best).

- Improve your memory system; *write it down.*

- Use different reading and study techniques for different material.

- Ask for assistance before it becomes a crisis.

- Plan on a minimum of one to two hours of study for each hour in class. (For example: A three-hour class requires three to six hours of study each week; a class that meets for one hour each day five days a week requires five to ten hours of study each week.)

Handout 9.4B. Tools for Academic Achievement. *Permission is granted to photocopy for group use.*

PSYCHOEDUCATIONAL GROUPS FOR ADULTS

Psychoeducational groups for adults have several advantages over groups for children and adolescents. Adults are less apt to be involuntary participants; most likely, they elected to attend. Adults will more often have specific objectives or learning they expect from the group, and are more aware of these expectations. Behavior, especially disruptive or aggressive behavior, is not usually a concern.

These advantages also carry some expectations for leaders. In order to meet these needs and expectations, leaders must be organized, plan well, and involve participants in setting goals.

Group composition and group size are of less concern than they were for children and adolescent groups. Helpers are useful for adult groups when group size rises above 20, however. It is generally most effective to divide a large group into small groups for discussion, exercises, and to promote interaction and involvement.

Length, duration, and number of sessions also are of less concern with groups for adults. Timing should be determined around availability of participants and the topic covered. Groups that have a topic of adequate interest for adults will attract and keep participants for a number of sessions over weeks and months.

Setting Goals and Objectives

Spend some time in the beginning of the group clarifying participants' goals, objectives, and expectations so that you can accommodate as many as possible. One way to do so is to have participants write their goals, objectives, and expectations on paper and then break into small groups, compile the lists on newsprint, post them on wall, discuss them, and come to some agreement on the most important ones for the group. A variation would be to divide into groups; brainstorm goals, objectives, and expectations; prioritize and write on newsprint; post on the wall; and discuss.

You may accurately anticipate the major goals, objectives, and expectations; but the primary outcome for any exercise is to promote involvement and commitment. Getting participants involved and excited encourages participation and promotes learning.

Environmental Concerns

Because adult group sessions tend to be held over a longer time span, you should pay attention to the comfort of participants. Adequate space for moving around and stretching is helpful, as is comfortable seating. Temperature control, a quiet atmosphere, adequate air exchange, and close availability of bathrooms also contribute to comfort.

Freedom from intrusion is as important for adults as it is for children and adolescents. Disruptions tend to focus attention away from the topic and interrupt input and interaction.

The following sample group program for adults includes a mini-lecture, two exercises, and two handouts.

PROGRAM 9.2. COMMUNICATIONS GROUP FOR ADULTS

Objectives: To identify five styles of ineffective communication; to increase awareness of personal bad listening habits; to learn seven strategies to improve listening habits; to learn attending behaviors; to learn core communication conditions

Materials: Newsprint, markers, paper, pens or pencils, copies of Handouts 9.5A and 9.5B, masking tape, felt-tip markers in a variety of colors sufficient for each participant or each group to have a set of basic colors

Time: One-day, six-hour workshop

Age/Education: Working professionals

Number of Participants: Unlimited (the example assumes 20 to 25)

Preparation: Review material on communication skills with particular attention to listening and nonverbal behaviors. Develop several examples of effective and ineffective communication for the target audience. Gather materials and organize space.

Sample Schedule for a One-Day Session

Activity	Strategy	Purpose(s)
Introduction, Overview	Didactic	Promote feelings of safety, set the agenda, orient participants to task
Get Acquainted	Game (not included)	Introduce group members to each other, promote universality, reduce isolation
Barriers to Communications	Discussion	Brainstorm and identify major barriers to effective communicating
Mini-Lecture on Listening and Responding	Lecture, discussion	Provide information, assess current levels of knowledge
My Listening Behavior	Exercise 9.5 & Handout 9.5A	Personalize information, increase awareness of personal listening behavior
Ineffective Communicators	Handout 9.5B	Gives examples of common ineffective communication styles
Misunderstandings	Exercise 9.6	Increase awareness of personal contributions to misunderstandings, practice other communications to reduce misunderstandings

Mini-Lecture: Listening and Responding

Prepare to Listen. Preparation for listening is primarily concerned with nonverbal behaviors. The other person must perceive you as present, interested, and caring when he or she talks to you in order for communication to be effective. The following behaviors communicate presence, interest, and caring.

Stop talking. You cannot talk and listen at the same time.

Face the speaker. Even slight turns away from the speaker can denote distraction or lack of interest. Maintain eye contact that is comfortable for you and for the other person.

Lean forward slightly. The position of your body also indicates interest. A slight forward lean and relaxed arms and legs convey presence and intent to attend to the other person.

Remove distractions. Do not engage in distracting behaviors such as reading, writing, fiddling with something (e.g., shuffling papers), or looking at TV.

Listening. In addition to attending behaviors, practice listening skills such as patience, empathy, and a focus on feelings, not just content. These are the skills that can help you understand what the speaker means, not just what he or she says. The meaning is the most important and major part of the message. Focusing on content loses about 90% of the message.

Have patience. You can listen and process faster than you can speak. Give the speaker time to fully express his or her thoughts. Do not interrupt, walk away, or become distracted.

Focus on feelings. Try to identify the major feelings the person is trying to communicate. Even orders convey feelings about the topic. Practice focusing on feelings, their contribution to understanding the message, and formulation of your response.

Have empathy. Empathy lets you understand the speaker's perspective. Understanding does not mean agreement, but it can provide a basis for working out disagreements. We are more apt to try to work out differences if we can feel the other person understands our viewpoint.

Increase your self-awareness. Knowing that your perceptual distortions influence what you choose to hear, understand, and omit helps you to be more objective when listening to others. The impact of the person's appearance and mannerisms, the topic, and your past experiences can all play a part in your ability to listen.

Prepare for Responding. Prepare to respond by using the difference between speaking time and hearing/thinking time to sort out issues, questions for clarification, and feelings. Thinking time is much faster than speaking time and can be used to formulate more effective responses.

Identify feelings. Focus on the underlying feelings contained in the message. These often are more important than the content. These feelings will form the first part of your response.

Monitor your feelings. If the speaker or his or her topic has triggered feelings for you, remind yourself that these are influencing your response and will impact what you choose to say as well as how you will say it.

Choose your words. Carefully formulate a response. Even when the topic appears to be clear-cut and straightforward, there are underlying feelings and messages you should take into account. There also may be parts of the message that need clarification, and the request for clarification should be part of the response.

Responding. All of the steps and activities above under "listening" can be done very quickly as thinking speed is considerably more rapid than speaking speed. Hence, you can prepare to respond as the other person is speaking as well as pay attention to what is being said and what is meant. Further, much of what is done in listening effectively is preparation for responding. Your responses will be more effective because you are more likely to have heard the real message and can phrase your response more effectively so that it too will be heard and understood.

Express heard cognitive message. Paraphrasing is one way to do this. Paraphrasing performs three functions: It shows interest in the speaker and that you want to understand his or her meaning; it conveys your understanding of what was said; and it allows the speaker to know if the intended message is coming through. Paraphrase by telling what the statement means to you, identifying a specific if the statement was general, suggesting an example to see if you understand what was meant, or extending a specific to a more generalized topic.

Express heard affective message. As noted before, the underlying message usually is a feeling. Try to name or label the feeling you identify. Be tentative unless the feeling is so intense there is little or no doubt as to what the speaker is feeling.

Ask clarifying questions. Preface questions with something like, "I want to make sure I understand you correctly. Do you mean ... ?" Do not bombard the speaker with questions, but ask enough so that you can make an appropriate response.

Refrain from argument or criticism. Even when you disagree with the speaker, you should try not to argue or criticize. This puts the speaker in a defensive position and effective communication ceases.

EXERCISE 9.5. MY LISTENING BEHAVIOR

Objectives: To determine ineffective listening behaviors; to understand ineffective ways of communicating

Materials: Copies of Handout 9.5A and 9.5B; pencils or pens

Time: 45 minutes

Age/Education: Adult working professionals

Number of Participants: 20 to 25

Preparation: Prepare chart with questions listed under procedure; prepare chart with list of ineffective communicators in Handout 9.5B; reproduce Handouts 9.5A and 9.5B; organize room.

Procedure: Introduce the exercise by describing how some behaviors, such as becoming distracted, interfere with the ability to listen well. Tell participants that sometimes habits they are not aware of make their listening less effective, and that sometimes they listen to some people but not to others. This exercise is designed to give an overview of the participants' listening behaviors.

Distribute both handouts and pencils and ask participants to fill out Handout 9.5A. Allow 5 to 10 minutes for this. Divide participants into groups of four or five members and ask them to discuss the following questions (write them on a chalkboard or poster paper ahead of time):

● Were you surprised at your score?

● Which ineffective listening behaviors do you use most often?

● Are there particular people or situations with whom you use more effective listening behaviors?

Allow 15 minutes for discussion.

In the large group, ask each small group to give a summary of its discussion.

Ask participants to look at Handout 9.5B. Go down the list and give an example and possible reaction for each. A list of possible negative reactions follows:

Drill sergeant	passive resistance (e.g., forget what was ordered)
Blamer	avoidance, resentment
Know-It-All	avoidance
Psychoanalyst	anger
Optimist	mistrust
Rescuer	resistance, desire for independence
Detective	anger, resentment, avoidance
Magician	frustration, hostility
Generalizer	lowered self-confidence, hostility
Accuser	avoidance, anger

Processing: The questions under "Procedure" are part of processing to encourage participants to begin to identify their patterns and behaviors of ineffective communicating. After presenting the categories in Handout 9.5B, focus the discussion on having participants identify other behaviors and feelings these communication styles arouse in the receiver, how often they use them, and strategies that would reduce or eliminate use.

My Listening Behavior

Directions: Recall your listening behavior over the past week, at home, work, and at social gatherings. Rate the extent to which you engaged in each of the following using the scale below.

5 = almost always; always   2 = seldom

4 = usually   1 = almost never; never

3 = sometimes

1. Called the subject uninteresting	5	4	3	2	1
2. Criticized the speaker's delivery or mannerisms	5	4	3	2	1
3. Became overstimulated by something the speaker says	5	4	3	2	1
4. Focused primarily on facts	5	4	3	2	1
5. Tried to mentally outline everything	5	4	3	2	1
6. Faked attention to the speaker	5	4	3	2	1
7. Became distracted	5	4	3	2	1
8. Avoided difficult material	5	4	3	2	1
9. Let emotionally laden words arouse personal antagonism	5	4	3	2	1
10. Engaged in daydreaming or thinking about something else	5	4	3	2	1

Total Score: _____

Scoring: Add the numbers checked to obtain your listening behavior score

40 - 50   =   You almost always use ineffective listening.

30 - 39   =   You frequently use ineffective listening.

20 - 29   =   You sometimes use ineffective listening. Look for a pattern of when you use ineffective listening.

Below 20 =   You may be able to improve, but you seldom use ineffective listening.

Handout 9.5A. My Listening Behavior. *Permission is granted to photocopy for group use.*

Ineffective Communicators

Drill Sergeant	Very authoritarian and likes to give orders
Blamer	Criticizes, condemns, moralizes, preaches, calls others names, uses words like *should* and *ought*
Know-It-All	Thinks he or she has all the answers and seldom checks to see if the answers fit the situation
Psychoanalyst	Ascribes reasons and motives to others with insufficient evidence
Optimist	Gushes with excessive optimism and avoids the real problem
Rescuer	Smothers others with patronizing "help" that robs them of their independence
Detective	So busy collecting facts that he or she neglects to listen to feelings; controls the conversation by battering others with questions
Magician	Denies the existence of a problem; tries to make it disappear by changing the topic
Generalizer	Uses words like *always* and *never* to describe behavior
Accuser	A name-caller who arouses hostility in others

Handout 9.5B. Ineffective Communicators. *Permission is granted to photocopy for group use.*

EXERCISE 9.6. MISUNDERSTANDINGS

Objectives: To increase awareness of personal contributions to misunderstandings; to develop more effective communications to reduce misunderstandings; to understand the role of emotions in misunderstandings

Materials: Newsprint 18" by 24" or larger for each participant; a set of felt-tip markers in a variety of colors for every two participants; masking tape

Time: 60 to 90 minutes

Age/Education: Adult working professionals

Number of Participants: Unlimited number of small groups, four to six members each

Preparation: Gather materials and organize room.

Procedure: Divide the large group into small groups, each around a table. Pass out materials. Introduce the exercise by asking participants to focus on a misunderstanding they have had that still concerns them in some way. The misunderstanding itself may have been resolved, but they may still wonder how it occurred or how to prevent it from happening again; or the misunderstanding may not be resolved and continues to affect the relationship. It may be between the participant and a coworker, a boss, a spouse, a child, a parent, or a friend.

Allow a period for reflection on the events that led up to the misunderstanding, the sequence of events during the misunderstanding, and subsequent actions. Participants may close their eyes. Ask that they try to reexperience any emotions associated with the misunderstanding.

After the reflection period, ask participants to select one scene that captures the essence of the misunderstanding and to draw it. They can use splashes of color to denote emotions.

Allow a sufficient time for drawing. Tell them when there are 3 to 5 minutes left for drawing. When the allotted time is up, allow 10 to 15 minutes for sharing the drawings in the small groups. After sharing, ask each group to select one drawing to be used in a role-play.

Each role-play is to be under the direction of the person whose drawing was selected or another volunteer. This person does not assume a role in the role-play; he or she only directs. The director assigns all roles, using the members in his or her group. Only major roles need be assigned, and roles do not have to be gender-specific. The director should select the person he or she feels could best play the role.

The director sets the scene, giving the players enough information to play their roles. Allow approximately 10 minutes for this preparation.

Have each group in turn role-play the misunderstanding. When they finish each role-play, ask the players to report on what they felt or experienced while playing the roles. Ask the director how accurate the role-play was and what feelings were aroused in him or her during the role-play.

Processing: After each group has had a chance to role-play, ask the participants to suggest ways in which the misunderstanding may have been prevented and strategies to prevent or lessen misunderstandings in the future.

Chapter 10

SOCIAL OR LIFE SKILLS TRAINING GROUPS

Social or life skills are those that smooth and enhance our interactions with others. They range from basic communication skills to complex ones, such as developing and maintaining relationships. Skills training groups teach people how to increase their effectiveness in relationships ranging from brief, impersonal interactions, such as buying an ice cream cone, to more complicated interactions, such as conflict management.

All of us learned what social skills we possess from direct and indirect teaching and modeling. Parents, other relatives, teachers, ministers, neighbors, and friends all participated in teaching us social or life skills. Some individuals, for one reason or another, do not receive adequate teaching or modeling early in life, and their daily functioning and interactions with others are impaired. This impairment promotes feelings of alienation and isolation, leading to a poor quality of life. Skills training usually involves a small group (5 to 10 members) that meets for several sessions over time, although some skills, such as communication skills, can be effectively presented in larger groups.

EFFECTIVENESS OF SOCIAL AND INTERPERSONAL SKILLS TRAINING

Goldstein and Glick (1987) surveyed studies on the effectiveness of interpersonal skills training for aggressive adolescent and preadolescent subjects. The subjects were adjudicated juvenile delinquents, status offenders, or high school students with a history of aggression. Study settings included psychiatric hospitals, residential institutions, schools, group homes, and clinics. Most studies used multiple groups, with members receiving instruction, modeling, role-play, and performance feedback. The groups focused on topics such as coping with criticism, negotiating, and problem-solving. The results for acquiring skills were consistently positive.

Psychological groups play an important role in social skills training. Indeed, these groups are the primary mode of delivery for such training. The following is a selected overview of studies on the effectiveness of this training, with an emphasis on the group. Studies were selected as samples of social skills training modes for children, for adolescents, and for adults with a variety of conditions.

A Meta-Analysis

In a meta-analysis of the effectiveness of cognitive-behavioral outcomes for children and adolescents, Durlak, Fuhrman, and Lampman (1991) found that 41% of studies employed group sessions, and approximately 75% used combinations of skills training with other techniques, such as role-play). The computed normative effect size (NES), an index of the comparison of treatment group with a normative or nonclinical group, showed that participants improved significantly. Their scores on such measures as anxiety, depression, and self-esteem not only significantly improved but rose to levels similar to those of children in the normative group.

Children

Skills training in nonhospital settings has evidence to support its efficacy. Much of the training has targeted conflict resolution for school children. These skills training programs generally involve communication skills, negotiating skills, recognizing options for behavior, and interpersonal helping.

- Moreau (1994) described a program for third-grade students that addressed development of social and conflict resolution skills. Teachers in a middle-class, suburban school identified the problems and participated in a training program to prepare them to teach conflict resolution skills. These skills were taught for 30 minutes daily over a six-week period. Results indicated that the children were better able to communicate with one another and to understand options available to them to solve their problems.

- Kamps, Leonard, Vernon, and Dugan (1992) investigated the effect of social skills groups on three autistic boys and their classmates in an integrated first-grade classroom. Results indicated increases in the frequency and duration of social interactions.

- Shure (1993) found that low-income preschoolers who were trained to think of alternative solutions to conflicts performed significantly better than their untrained peers at controlling impulsive behaviors in the classroom.

- Weist, Vannatta, and Wayland (1993) described the outcomes for a group training program for sexually abused girls, ages 8 through 11. Teachers reported improved perceived academic competence, peer functioning, appearance, and global self-concept following the training program.

Adolescents

In a study of the effects of cooperative learning and conflict resolution programs in an alternative inner-city high school in New York, Khattri (1991) concluded that both strategies were useful and valid for students' academic learning and psychological development.

College Students

Swell (1992) studied an instructional program for college students that focused on self-esteem, values identification, conflict management, and positive reinforcement. Results of the study of 394 first-year students showed significant improvement for participants when matched with a control group.

Stein, Cislo, and Ward (1994) reported that a one-semester course on developing social skills for undergraduates who would be working with psychiatrically disabled people increased the students' social networks, attitudes toward people with psychiatric disabilities, interpersonal self-efficacy, and social skills.

Psychiatric Patients

Fine, Forth, Gilbert, and Haley (1991) compared social skills training and therapeutic support groups for 66 depressed adolescents (ages 13 to 17). Self-support and semistructured clinical interviews for depression, measures of self-concept, and cognitive distortions were used to measure outcomes. The therapeutic support group participants showed significantly greater reductions in clinical depression and significant increases in self-concept. However, these differences were no longer evident at the nine-month follow-up. The therapeutic support group participants maintained their improvement; and the social skills training group participants caught up.

Douglas and Mueser (1990) described outcomes for a social skills training program held over a three-year period at an acute care psychiatric hospital. Data from 286 patients who participated for the entire three years, and from an additional 200 who had at least two sessions, showed a significant improvement in skills even for those who had brief participation.

Managers

Hall and Cockburn (1990) reported on managers who had participated in a learner-centered modeling program to increase management skills. A one-year follow-up study showed that the effectiveness of skills training was increased 10% to 70%. The focus for the action learning was interpersonal skills.

LEADING A SOCIAL OR LIFE SKILLS TRAINING GROUP

Prior to the start of a skills training group, the leader should glean as much information as possible about the potential group members and their needs for training. This information can be obtained from interviews or surveys with group members or with those who have considerable contact with members (e.g., teachers) or from written records. There are times when skills training is sought for a general objective and little information is available about specific needs of participants. For example, teachers in an elementary school may request human relations skills training. Little is known about specific members; however, some information can be inferred to help plan for such a group.

The next step is to search the literature for studies, books, or articles that present data and ideas on effective strategies with the intended audience and the skills deficits. Having some notion about what is effective, what is not, and differing strategies helps you choose from a wide array of strategies. Two data bases that focus on studies and reports are *ERIC* and *Psyc.Lit.*

There are published programs that combine strategies into cohesive presentations. Some may be adequate for your intended audience, but it is difficult to fully develop a program that fits any or all audiences. If you choose to use such a program, be sure to thoroughly review and assess it first.

When feasible, you should assess the participants' present level of functioning. This can be accomplished through personal interviews or through the use of established valid behavioral rating scales or procedures. You should assess strengths as well as deficits, as existing strengths can be used as building blocks for social skills development.

Basic techniques for social or life skills training include teaching, modeling, and behavior rehearsal. Each technique is discussed below.

Teaching

Basic instructional strategies presented in chapter 2 can be followed for teaching social skills. However, these groups tend to have fewer members, and you should make only minimal use of lectures to present material. Focus more on presenting a few major concepts that can be discussed among members while you inject new ideas, correct misinformation, and identify gaps in learning.

Another useful strategy is to provide relevant books and articles around the topics. Use simple reading material, as it is more likely to be read. Become familiar with children's and young adult books at your local public library, as these address many topics covered in social skills training. You can best choose materials if you know the reading levels of your participants. If you do not have access to that information, you should have a variety of reading materials at all levels. It may be useful to compile a list of books on many reading levels for your reference, and to distribute that list to participants.

Modeling

Modeling is an important part of teaching. You should model desired behaviors and lead by example. Using good leadership and communication skills with the group demonstrates more effective ways of behaving and relating.

Another way to present modeling is through the use of media. Look for videos that present visual demonstrations of effective and ineffective behaviors. Maintain a list of related videos or catalogues that feature them.

A frequently overlooked source for modeling is a group member. You should be alert to the presence of social skills in the group. Capitalize on these resources by identifying them openly in the group. Do not focus only on undesired behaviors; reinforce desired ones.

Behavior Rehearsal

Behavior rehearsal is similar to role-play where a situation is acted out. The differences are that role-play is usually about a past event about which the actor is trying to gain understanding, whereas in behavior rehearsal the event has not yet occurred and the actor is practicing new behavior.

To set up a behavior rehearsal, first identify the new behavior that will be rehearsed, the situation where it is needed, and others who will be or might be present. Ask for volunteers to assume the other roles and give them enough information that they can help provide a nearly accurate situation.

After the situation has been performed with the actor assuming the new behavior, the discussion can focus on feelings experienced by all the players with particular emphasis on the feelings of the actor playing the new behavior. Other players and group member who did not participate can give the actor feedback on perceived effectiveness.

Following is a social skills training group program designed for adolescents. This program includes seven exercises, two mini-lectures, and three handouts, used over eight sessions. It assumes a small number of participants.

PROGRAM 10.1. SOCIAL SKILLS GROUP

Focus: Building strengths

Objectives: To increase awareness of personal assets; to help participants perceive the positive aspects of characteristics that have been criticized by others; to develop an action plan for building on existing strengths

Materials: Handouts 10.2A, 10.2B, and 10.5; pens and pencils; 5" x 8" index cards; glue sticks; sandwich bags; paper; newsprint; masking tape; medium-size boxes; felt-tip markers in a variety of colors; crayons or oil pastels in a variety of colors

Time: One 60- to 90-minute session each week for eight weeks

Age/Education: 13- to 17-years-olds; no more than a two-year age difference between members

Number of Participants: Six to eight per group

Preparation: Reproduce Handouts 10.2A, 10.2B, and 10.5. Review literature on building self-esteem. Interview participants if possible; if not possible, try to find out as much as possible about participants from teachers and counselors. Secure a room with appropriate privacy, that has tables that can be used for group activities, and that is free from outside noise and distractions.

Note: Some of the activities can be used with larger groups when used in isolation, that is, when they are not part of a program such as the one described here. When used in a larger group, opportunities for sharing are reduced and the time needed is increased. The time limits presented here are for smaller groups.

Sample Schedule for an Eight-Session Program

Session	Activity
Session 1	Introductions; Exercise 10.1. "Getting to Know You" Game; Overview of group (not included); Goal setting and review of rules (not included)
Session 2	Summary of previous session; Exercise 10.2. I Want ... , I Need ... ; Mini-Lecture: Personal Management Skills, and Handout 10.2A
Session 3	Unfinished business from previous session; Attitude Skills Survey (Handout 10.2B) and discussion; Exercise 10.3. Box of Me
Session 4	Unfinished business from previous session; Processing for Exercise 10.3. Box of Me
Session 5	Unfinished business from previous session; Exercise 10.4. The Positive Side of Criticism; Mini-Lecture: Becoming More Effective
Session 6	Unfinished business from previous session; Exercise 10.5. Developing Personal Affirmations; 15 Qualities of an Effective Person (Handout 10.5), plus discussion
Session 7	Unfinished business from previous session; Goal check-up (not included); Introduction of termination of group (not included); Exercise 10.6. Brainstorming
Session 8	Unfinished business from previous session; Exercise 10.7. Sketch of My Future; Termination issues (not included); Closing exercise (not included)

EXERCISE 10.1. "GETTING TO KNOW YOU" GAME

Objectives: To help group members get acquainted; to focus on important components of self, especially strengths

Materials: 5" by 8" cards for each member; glue sticks; a sandwich bag with 10 to 15 cut-out pictures; sample mini-collage; tables or other hard surfaces for preparing the mini-collages; chairs in a circle for processing

Time: 30 minutes for construction and processing

Age/Education: 6 years old and above

Number of Participants: Unlimited

Preparation: The group leader should prepare the bags and sample mini-collage in advance of the session.

Procedure: Tell members that this is a get-acquainted activity. Since one objective for the group is to increase awareness of personal assets, the activity will ask each member present some of his or her assets. Use the sample mini-collage to illustrate.

Instruct members to use the pictures in their bags to construct mini-collages on their cards. The pictures should be symbolic of their strengths, assets, things they do well, and accomplishments. They are free to exchange pictures if they want.

Allow approximately 10 minutes for construction.

Processing: Ask members return to the circle and talk about the symbols in their mini-collages. Allow only clarifying questions and positive comments. Try to highlight and emphasize strengths and commonalities.

EXERCISE 10.2. I WANT ... , I NEED ...

Objectives: To increase awareness of the difference between wants and needs; to focus attention on personal wants and needs

Materials: A sheet of paper with a line lengthwise down the middle for each participant; pencils or pens; large sheets of newsprint or a flip chart; masking tape

Time: 30 minutes

Age/Education: 6th grade reading level and above

Number of Participants: 30 to 35

Preparation: Gather materials.

Procedure: Ask participants to list all of their wants on the left side of their sheet of paper. Have them label that column "Wants." Allow 3 to 5 minutes for completion. Once lists have been generated, allow 10 minutes for members to read their lists aloud. You can tabulate the items on a sheet of newsprint posted on the wall. Tabulate the items into the following categories: relationships, objects, accomplishments, spiritual, emotional. Add other categories as they emerge. Discuss any commonalities that appear and the most frequently chosen categories.

Have members list all their needs in the next column, labeled "Needs." Ask them to star (*) any wants that are also needs. Ask members read their needs lists aloud, then tabulate these into the same categories as "Wants."

Processing: Discuss any commonalities and most frequent categories. Ask members to summarize what they see as similar and as different in their personal wants and needs.

Mini-Lecture: Personal Management Skills

What kind of person are you right now? What kind of person do you want to be in 5 or 10 years? Beyond that? You can help yourself become the kind of person you want to be. While others can help and support you in this endeavor, and life circumstances can have a significant impact, *you* are the most important part of the outcome.

There are five personal management skills you can use to help you become the person you want to be. These attitudes and behaviors can help you make decisions about practically everything, from what career to pursue to which activities to engage in. While I briefly describe each one, I want you to think of examples that are personal for you.

Valuing means investing in yourself. When you value someone you take care of him or her and use whatever resources you have to make sure his or her needs are met. Make the same investment of time, energy, and resources in yourself. Take care of your physical, emotional, psychological, and spiritual needs. Others can help, but you must invest in yourself.

Planning is a critical life skill. Few activities are more important than this one. You should set both short-term (one to six months) and long-term goals (these may be years in the future). Having goals gives you a sense of direction and can suggest strategies for getting where you want to go. Remember, if you don't know where you're going, you may end up somewhere else.

Commitment to yourself is important as well. Knowing your abilities, aptitudes, and goals—and valuing them—is crucial. However, you also must believe in yourself and have faith that you can and will succeed in becoming the person you want to be. Belief can be difficult to maintain sometimes, especially when you make mistakes or others criticize you. No matter how difficult it may be, keep faith in yourself.

Priorities are important in successful time management *and in successful personal management*. Prioritizing allows us to focus our time, energy, and resources on the most important things instead of allowing them to be wasted. Determine what is important for you and stay focused on it.

Pacing yourself is a valuable skill. Anything worth accomplishing takes time. Becoming the person you want to be is a process that will take time. Become comfortable working toward your goal. You will get there one step at a time if you remember what is important and work on that, believe in yourself, know your goals, and invest in yourself.

Personal Management Skills

Valuing yourself	Invest in you.
Planning	Set goals for now and for the future.
Committing	Believe in yourself.
Setting priorities	Stay focused on what is important.
Pacing	Take it one step at a time.

Handout 10.2A. Personal Management Skills. *Permission is granted to photocopy for group use.*

Attitude Skills Survey

Directions: Rate the degree to which you possess these attitude skills using the following scale.

5 = Always; a great deal	2 = Seldom; on occasion
4 = Usually; to a considerable extent	1 = Never; almost never
3 = Sometimes; to some extent	NA = Does not apply to me

Ability to be honest with myself: _____

Creative: _____

Appreciative of beauty: _____

Willing to learn: _____

Present-centered: _____

Capacity for happiness and joy: _____

Courage to try new ways of being and behaving: _____

Spontaneous: _____

High self-regard: _____

Self-acceptance: _____

Capacity for intimacy: _____

Sensitive to my own needs and feelings: _____

Accepting of both pleasant and uncomfortable feeling in myself: _____

Score: _____

Handout 10.2B. Attitude Skills Survey. *Permission is granted to photocopy for group use.*

EXERCISE 10.3. BOX OF ME

Objectives: To help members focus on positive aspects of themselves; to increase awareness of personal assets; to learn to talk about strengths

Materials: Medium-sized boxes (e.g., 6" by 9" gift boxes); other materials supplied by group members

Time: Unlimited, as this is a homework assignment

Age/Education: All ages

Number of Participants: Unlimited

Preparation: Gather medium-sized boxes (e.g., 6" by 9" gift boxes).

Procedure: Introduce the exercise by asking members to list 10 of their assets, strengths, and positive aspects. Ask them to reflect on what symbols, things, or pictures illustrate their list. Pass out the boxes and tell them to collect anything that would illustrate the 10 items on their list, plus any others that occur to them; have them put the items in the box to bring to the next session. They may wish to collect photographs, medals or other awards, items that symbolize values, or anything that can be used as a symbol.

Processing: At the next session allow enough time for members to share parts of their collections. Focus on the feelings they experienced while compiling the collections and those they experience when presenting to the group.

EXERCISE 10.4. THE POSITIVE SIDE OF CRITICISM

Objectives: To help participants perceive strengths; to increase awareness of personal strengths

Materials: Paper and pens or pencils for each participant

Time: 20 to 30 minutes

Age/Education: 6th grade reading level and above

Number of Participants: 30 to 35

Preparation: Gather materials.

Procedure: Tell participants that embedded in almost every criticism or perceived weakness is a strength. Each of us needs to capitalize on our strengths as well as seek to overcome any perceived weakness.

On one side of the paper, have participants list 8 to 10 criticisms they have of themselves or that others have of them. They do not have to agree with the criticism, just to list it.

After the lists have been generated, ask participants to look at each item and list on the other side of the page all strengths they see in that criticism. Post some examples of embedded strengths. For example:

Criticism	Strength
Take things personally	Sensitive to others' perceptions
Lazy	Relaxed
Talk too much	Seek to connect and communicate with others

If members have trouble perceiving a strength, you can make suggestions. Members may be able to help each other with suggestions.

Processing: After they have generated their lists, give members time to share them. If the group is too large for each member to share, divide into smaller groups.

Allow enough time for each member to share some part of his or her list. Call time and process the experience by asking a few questions: What was difficult? What was easy? How hard was it to see a strength? How do they feel about the criticisms after doing the exercise?

Mini-Lecture: Becoming More Effective

We all have a tendency to focus more on weaknesses than on strengths. Weaknesses are those things about which we feel shame: We think we are flawed, and there is little we can do to change things. We may feel that our time and energy should be spent on remediating those weaknesses.

Some of our perceptions of weaknesses are generated by others' criticisms and some arise from within us. Parents, siblings, and others we care about give us feedback on how they perceive us, and this is often in the form of criticism, which we then take to heart. Consequently, we begin to feel ashamed and guilty. Worse are the criticisms we have of ourselves, those that arise from the notion that we should not make mistakes or that we should be perfect. Both forms of criticisms can be beneficial, but often they cause us much discomfort.

However, there are some things we can do to be more effective. In Exercise 10.4, we focused on seeing strengths in criticisms. Other strategies that can enhance a sense of self-efficacy and promote effectiveness are relabeling, surrendering, recognizing personal limitations, using our imaginations, and practicing affirmations.

Relabeling is very much like seeing the positive side of criticisms. When you feel put down, unworthy, or ashamed, try to relabel the event and see the positive side or strength that is embedded in it. Try not to look only at what you did *not* do or what you do *not* have; instead, look at what is positive and good about the event or perception.

Surrendering refers to changing what you can and letting go of the rest. Few things are all-or-nothing events, but we often find ourselves thinking that there is nothing positive in a situation. Try to focus on what is possible to change, and then *let go of the rest*. Do not obsess over those things you cannot change.

Recognizing personal limitations is a part of maturity. This does not mean you should sit back and avoid taking any risks or trying anything difficult. It does mean that you should judge yourself realistically and accept yourself for who you are. Knowing your limit and limitations and accepting yourself in spite of *or because of them* is healthy and mature.

Use your imagination to visualize what could and can be. What if you were to work hard at becoming what you want to be? How would you see yourself? Imagine that you could be whatever you wanted to be, given your abilities and physical self. What then?

Giving yourself affirmations is another positive and important strategy. The difference between a winner and a loser is in the losing: The winner says, "I can do better," then goes out and works harder. The loser sulks and says, "I lost." Tell yourself you have strengths, you can do, you will try, and that whatever happens, you will continue to accept yourself.

EXERCISE 10.5. DEVELOPING PERSONAL AFFIRMATIONS

Objectives: To develop list of personal assets that can form the basis for self-affirming statements; to focus on strengths

Materials: Paper and pen for each participant

Time: 30 to 60 minutes

Age/Education: 3rd grade reading level and above

Number of Participants: 30 to 35

Preparation: Gather materials.

Procedure: Review Handout 10.5., 15 Qualities of the Effective Person. Ask participants to make a list of 10 to 12 phrases or words to complete the sentence, "I am ... ." Ask them to focus on their positive qualities, those things they do well or about which they feel a sense of accomplishment. Then, allow time for each member to read aloud or to share with at least one other member.

Next, have members generate another list to finish the sentence, "I can ... ." This list should enumerate the abilities they possess and the steps they can take to enhance existing strengths, develop new ones, or overcome a perceived deficiency. Allow time for sharing.

Processing: Processing should focus on helping members highlight the positive parts of their lists. Have them rewrite their lists into self-affirming statements that they can refer back to whenever they need a pick-me-up.

15 Qualities of an Effective Person

1. An ability to be present-centered

2. A clear sense of purpose and direction

3. A caring and loving attitude

4. Well-organized and able to accomplish much

5. Intellectually sharp and able to handle quantities of information

6. A sense of humor

7. Experiences and can express a wide range of emotions

8. Accepting of his or her limitations and mistakes

9. Practices self-care

10. Can be assertive when necessary

11. Assumes responsibility for his or her own life

12. Has a deep commitment to a cause outside of him- or herself

13. Willing to take psychological risks

14. Allows him- or herself to be creative

15. Is aware of personal values

Handout 10.5. 15 Qualities of an Effective Person. *Permission is granted to photocopy for group use.*

EXERCISE 10.6. BRAINSTORMING

Objectives: To increase awareness of commonalities among group members; to develop strategies for overcoming barriers to enhancing of personal assets; to learn to capitalize on existing strengths

Materials: Newsprint for posting on the wall as a flip chart; felt-tip markers; masking tape; prepared list of strategies on newsprint—Relabel, Surrender, Recognize, Imagine, Give Self-Affirmations (see mini-lecture on Becoming More Effective)

Time: 30 to 40 minutes

Age/Education: 6th grade and above

Number of Participants: 30 to 35

Preparation: Gather materials; prepare list of strategies to becoming more effective.

Procedure: Divide the group into pairs and give each pair a sheet of newsprint and a felt-tip pen. Scatter pairs around the room where they can write, either on tables, on the floor, or on paper posted on the wall.

Direct pairs to brainstorm barriers and constraints individuals face when they are trying to develop, use, or expand their personal assets. Barriers might include friends making fun of them, others looking at them funny, feeling different, and so on. They are not to discuss the items, just write them on the newsprint. They should write as many as they can in five minutes.

Processing: After lists have been generated, post them on the wall. Show the group the prepared lists of strategies and briefly review them. Then review the items generated in brainstorming and have members talk about how the strategies can be used to overcome the barriers and constraints. You should write the strategy beside the barrier. As the group lists strategies, focus the discussion on what would be difficult about using the designated strategy.

EXERCISE 10.7. SKETCH OF MY FUTURE

Objectives: To help members formulate goals for their personal development; to summarize personal learning from the group sessions

Materials: Large sheets of newsprint; a set of felt-tip markers, crayons, or oil pastels for each pair of group members

Time: 40 minutes

Age/Education: 3rd grade and above

Number of Participants: 30 to 35 (works best with a small group of no more than 10 members)

Preparation: Gather materials; insure adequate drawing space for each participant.

Procedure: Distribute two sheets of newsprint for each member and a set of markers for each two members. Introduce the exercise by briefly summarizing the material that presented in the preceding exercises.

Direct members to close their eyes and to imagine they are 5 years older. What are they doing? How do they look and feel? What are they most proud of in terms of personal development? Allow a short period for reflection and then have members open their eyes and draw what they saw. Drawings can be realistic or symbolic. Have members title their drawings.

Ask members to close their eyes and fast forward 10 years. Go through the same process.

Post both drawings for each member and have each member describe both drawings.

Processing: Process the experience by having members focus on their identified strengths. If the group is larger than 10, ask for volunteers to share what emerged as strengths. In a smaller group, everyone can contribute.

Chapter 11

WORK-RELATED PSYCHOEDUCATIONAL GROUPS

Work-related psychoeducational groups may be called professional development workshops or seminars, managerial training, or organizational development training. These groups are intended to help workers at all levels learn new skills or processes that will increase productivity. The primary focus usually is on workers learning better ways to perform their jobs more effectively and efficiently.

Work-related psychoeducational groups typically are designed for adults. Some focus on teaching adolescents work-related skills, but these are more often found in schools or other training facilities, such as group homes and vocational schools.

LEADER TASKS

Planning for the group begins with getting a clear understanding of the goals and objectives. Since these groups usually are initiated by an employer, the leader must consult with the appropriate officials and determine what outcomes are expected, get a description of the intended audience, find a time for the sessions, and determine space needs and other financial considerations. Following is a short list of questions to explore when planning such a group.

What are the primary outcomes expected? What does the employer expect participants to know or be able to do as a result of the group?

Who are the participants? You will need to know their ages, educational levels, and average time in present positions—that is, new on the job or long-term. You will want to know how many participants you will have and whether the group is homogenous or a mix of managers and subordinates. One final consideration is whether will there be primarily males or females in the group, or a mixture.

What time is available? Be explicit about the number of hours the group will last: For example, say three hours rather than half a day, which could be either three or four hours. If there are several sessions planned, will there be the consistent time for the group to meet?

What facilities will be used? Will the group be held on-site, at the organization's facilities at another site, in rented facilities, or in some other place?

What are the funding concerns? Will you have sufficient funds to cover helpers' stipends, the cost of materials, copying, renting movies or equipment, and refreshments?

Do you need to submit a written plan or proposal before the group is developed? Is a follow-up or evaluation required?

Other leader tasks in planning include developing a written plan, preparing helpers, and reviewing the facilities.

A Written Plan

Even if the organization does not require you to submit a plan or proposal, it is helpful to write one. The plan is your guide to organizing the group and can serve as a checklist to ensure smooth running of the group. The written plan also is a guide for your helpers. They can better understand what will be done and what they need to do.

Your written plan should include, but is not limited to, the items in Table 11.1. It also is helpful to designate the responsible person and date by which the item is to be completed.

TABLE 11.1
A Sample Plan

Task	Person	Completion Date
Consult with organization	Brown	January 16
Literature review	Brown	January 20
Develop goals and objectives	Brown	January 30
Review goals and objectives with organization	Brown	February 10
Review available materials	Brown	February 10
Meet with helpers	Brown	February 10
Visit facilities	Brown	February 12
Develop materials	Brown	February 16
Develop schedule	Brown	February 16
Type and copy materials	Helper	February 25
Arrange for needed equipment	Helper	February 25
Order needed materials	Helper	February 25
Arrange for refreshments	Helper	February 25
Prepare packages of materials	Helper	February 25

Preparing Your Helpers

Preparing helpers is an important task. Helpers free the leader to concentrate on the participants and accomplishment of goals and objectives. Helpers need to understand the overall plan as well as their particular jobs. Some helper tasks are listed in the sample plan above, and they perform other tasks in the group. When assigning tasks, be sure to tell helpers the completion date, where resources such as copying machines are located and how to access them, and how materials will be paid for.

Helpers also need to know what time they are expected to begin and end on the day of the group and what they are to do during the sessions. Helpers can distribute materials, set up equipment, make sure refreshments are as ordered and on time, answer questions participants have about directions, and make the leader aware of glitches and participants' concerns.

Knowing Your Space

Reviewing the facilities is crucial. Environmental concerns of space, furniture, freedom form intrusion, and restroom availability are some of the basics that need attention. If media is to be used, location of outlets, screen placement, video placement, etc., also needs review by the leader. Scoping out the facilities helps the group run smoothly and is one less thing to worry about during the session.

Developing Goals and Objectives

Developing realistic goals and objectives cannot be overemphasized. Remember that little or nothing is known about the participants to help you determine what and how much they can learn. You probably will not know about participants' prior preparation, readiness, motivation, or level of reading and critical thinking ability. However, there are some basic guidelines you can use when developing objectives based on assumptions about the intended audience.

You should assume that participants want to know how to do their jobs better, that clearly relating the group's tasks to their jobs promotes participation, and that participants want a sense of accomplishment upon completion of the group. These assumptions suggest that objectives should be concrete and specific to the participants' jobs, that the intended learning should be spelled out in unambiguous terms, and that enough new material should be introduced to allow participants to feel a sense of accomplishment.

Developed goals and objectives should be reviewed with participants during the overview of the group, along with the proposed schedule. It is unlikely there will be any objections or new ideas, but reviewing what is planned and asking for reactions and input promotes involvement and commitment.

Scheduling Events

Plan for activities, breaks, discussion, everything. Estimate how much time each event will take and plan for continual adjustment to the schedule, except for beginning, ending, and breaks. Do not change these times except under extreme conditions. End discussions by noting that they will be picked up where left off but that it is important to have the scheduled break.

It can be difficult to estimate time needed for an activity even when you have done the activity before. All groups are different, and what may take 30 minutes with one group can run on to a hour with another because of important material or learning that emerges and should be explored. Conversely, an activity that takes 30 to 40 minutes for most groups may be completed in 15 minutes. You need considerable flexibility to conduct psychoeducational groups.

Be sure to review the schedule with your helpers and to have copies for participants. The events on the schedule also serve as the primary points to develop the evaluation. Participants have an easier time rating when the evaluated events are the same as the scheduled ones.

Below are some basic guidelines for scheduling.

- Do not scheduling an extended discussion just before a break, a video or movie just after lunch, or an energizing activity at termination.

- Complete all exercises before breaks or lunch; do not carry them over into another time slot.

- Keep your mini-lectures short, and hand out lists of the primary points.

- Schedule an energizing participatory exercise or game for early afternoon.

- If you use guest speakers, let them deliver the lead-off or keynote theme. Schedule them first, not just before or just after lunch.

Using Media

Media include transparencies, slides, video and movies, audio, and computer-generated graphics. If you are presenting data in this way, have it professionally prepared, and make sure you or your helper know how to run the equipment. Presentations should be brief, concise, easily heard and seen from the back of the room, have good sound quality, and delivered in an interesting way. Make extensive use of clip art, cartoons, appropriate jokes, and art work. These add and help maintain interest.

Following are materials and a plan for a work-related group on time management. The program includes 6 exercises, 3 mini-lectures, and 11 handouts.

PROGRAM 11.1. TIME MANAGEMENT

Objectives: To learn effective ways to manage time and to increase achievement of tasks; to increase awareness of personal use of time and potentials for more effective use; to learn to plan, prioritize, and stay focused on short-term and long-term goals; to identify personal time wasters and those related to managerial functions; to learn to plan and conduct meetings

Materials: Paper, pens or pencils, newsprint, masking tape, markers

Time: Full day

Age/Education: Employed adults in managerial and supervisory positions

Number of Participants: 35

Preparation: Gather materials; prepare examples; develop mini-lectures; organize space.

Contents for a Work-Related Group

Time Associations	Exercise & Handout 11.1
Setting Goals	Exercise & Handout 11.2
Daily Planning	Mini-Lecture
My Work Plan	Exercise & Handout 11.3
Reconstructing a Day	Exercise 11.4 & Handout 11.4A
Categories of Time Use	Handout 11.4B
Analysis of My Tasks	Exercise 11.5 & Handout 11.5A
Some Time Wasters Related to Time Management Functions	Handout 11.5B
Time Wasters and Management Functions	Handout 11.5C
Strategies to Address Time Wasters	Handout 11.5D
Paperwork	Mini-Lecture
Meetings	Mini-Lecture
Tools for Time Management	Handout 11.6A
Some Basic Time Management Strategies	Handout 11.6B

EXERCISE 11.1 TIME ASSOCIATIONS

Objectives: To help participants focus on their feelings about time; to emphasize personal associations for time and related issues; to clarify present attitudes about time

Materials: A copy of Handout 11.1. Time Associations; a pencil or pen for each participant; newsprint; markers; masking tape

Time: 30 minutes

Age/Education: 8th grade reading level and above

Number of Participants: 35

Preparation: Develop a list of four to five time associations with categories as a model (see directions below).

Procedure: Distribute Handout 11.1 and pens. Ask participants to quickly list all words, phrases, and feelings that come to mind when they hear the word *time*. Allow 5 to 7 minutes for completion.

Ask if any participant would like to read his or her list aloud. Usually there will be several volunteers. You can also begin by reading your own list and then asking for volunteers.

Next, have participants categorize their lists and share them in small groups. Finally, do large group processing.

Words and phrases on lists can be categorized using one of the following sets: positive or negative, passive or active, rewarding or punishing, pleasant or unpleasant, adjective or verb, and so on. A prepared example can be demonstrated. An example of categorizing as positive or negative is shown below:

Association	Category
rushed	negative
not enough	negative
on my hands	negative
goes by	positive

Processing: Have participants count the number or percentage of words and phrases in each category. The categories are polarities that highlight intensity of personal associations. Some words or phrases may fall into a neutral category. There is no need to force them into a category, as one purpose is to highlight personal feelings about time.

After calculations, ask for volunteers to report their major categories, which can be tabulated on newsprint and posted where participants can see it. This allows the group to become more aware of similarities among members as well as providing a focus for further processing.

Next, ask participants for ideas on what contributes to the categorizations. For example, what factors contribute to categorizing associations as positive or negative? If the group is relatively small—less than 35—it may be possible to further categorize these responses as under the individual's control or controlled by outside forces. This is helpful, as the most useful part of the time management group focuses on variables the individual can control.

Time Associations

Directions: List all the feelings, clichés, associations, or thoughts that come into your mind when you think of the word *time*. For example:

Association	Category
1. Clock _____	_____
2. _____	_____
3. _____	_____
4. _____	_____
5. _____	_____
6. _____	_____
7. _____	_____
8. _____	_____
9. _____	_____
10. _____	_____
11. _____	_____
12. _____	_____
13. _____	_____
14. _____	_____
15. _____	_____
16. _____	_____
17. _____	_____
18. _____	_____
19. _____	_____
20. _____	_____

Handout 11.1. Time Associations. *Permission is granted to photocopy for group use.*

EXERCISE 11.2. SETTING GOALS

Objectives: To develop a list of long-term and short-term goals; to develop a plan for attaining the goals; to learn a planning process

Materials: Handout 11.2; pen or pencil for each participant; newsprint; masking tape

Time: 1 to 2 hours

Age/Education: 8th grade reading level and above

Number of Participants: 35

Preparation: Gather materials and organize room so you can observe how fast or slow participants are working. Prepare and post newsprint with three headings shown at the top—Career/Work, Home/Family/ Relationships, and Personal Development.

Procedure: Distribute Handout 11.2 and pencils or pens. Introduce the exercise with the following statement and questions.

"If you don't know where you are going, you'll probably end up somewhere else."
—David Campbell (1974)

Questions to ponder and answer:

1. Do you have *in writing* short-term goals for work, home, and personal development?

2. Do you have your long-term goals in writing?

3. Can you list all the steps necessary for you to attain your goals?

4. Can you list all of the barriers that lie between you and your goals?

   After introducing the questions, tell participants that you will guide them in filling out Handout 11.2. Read each section and allow time for participants to write answers.

Planning to Achieve. The most important task in managing your time is planning. Most people have only vague ideas of their goals. Even if they can identify a career or work goal with some specificity, they have failed to identify goals in other areas of their lives. It is not enough to have goals in only one part of your life. If your time is to be managed effectively and you are to feel productive, you need a goal for each major area of your life. This will help ensure that significant portions of your lives are not neglected but are focused on, worked toward, and achieved.

> **Goals**—Develop a long-term and a short-term goal for your career, for home and family, and for your personal development. Think of long-term as 5 to 10 years in the future and short-term as from less than one year to four years in the future. Write words or phrases for the goals in the space provided.

Note: Watch participants as they complete this section, and when most seem finished, begin the next section noting that they can return to finish it later.

> **What Is Needed to Attain Each Goal**—Look at your goals and list what you need to do, need to obtain, or need to have happen to reach your goals. Things such as additional education, resolution of conflict or health problems, or a new home are some examples.

> **Barriers**—List major barriers that can keep you from reaching your goal. Examples of barriers include a lack of money, personal qualities such as a tendency to procrastinate, lack of opportunities for advancement at one's present job, etc. For some goals, there may be no barriers, in which case what is needed is the decision to just do it.

> **Criteria of Success**—How will you know you are successful? What specifically will happen? List these. Now that you have some idea of what you are trying to accomplish and have your goals in writing, you are more likely to accomplish them. Remember, goals can be achieved; once they are achieved, new goals must be set. Confidence comes with setting and achieving goals. Work on your goals daily when possible and resolve that no week will pass without your addressing some goal-related task.

> **Processing:** Processing focuses on having participants read what they wrote and determine what was most useful, surprising, or reaffirming for them. As each tells the group one or more of these, list them on the posted newsprint prepared in advance with the three headings.

Setting Goals

Directions: Answer each of the following questions as completely as possible. The group leader will provide guidance as you work through the exercise.

My Goals   Long-Term Goals   Short-Term Goals

Career/Work: _____   _____

    _____   _____

Home/Family/
Relationships: _____   _____

    _____   _____

Personal
Development: _____   _____

    _____   _____

What I Need to Do to Attain My Goals

          Long-Term   Short-Term

Career/Work: _____   _____

    _____   _____

Home/Family/
Relationships: _____   _____

    _____   _____

Personal
Development: _____   _____

    _____   _____

    _____   _____

Barriers to Attaining My Goals

	Long-Term	Short-Term
Career/Work:	_____	_____
	_____	_____
Home/Family/ Relationships:	_____	_____
	_____	_____
Personal Development:	_____	_____
	_____	_____

Criteria for Success in Attaining My Goals

	Long-Term	Short-Term
Career/Work:	_____	_____
	_____	_____
Home/Family/ Relationships:	_____	_____
	_____	_____
Personal Development:	_____	_____
	_____	_____
	_____	_____

Handout 11.2. Setting Goals. *Permission is granted to photocopy for group use.*

Mini-Lecture: Daily Planning

In order to accomplish your goals, you need to plan on a daily basis. By planning on a daily basis, you will stay focused on your goals and engage in those activities that will help you achieve them. Daily planning keeps you from getting bogged down in unproductive tasks. A daily plan is not rigid but allows for flexibility and change. Your daily plan should include the following:

1. **A list of things to do.** Do not trust your memory; write down what you need or want to do daily. Guard against listing trivia; list the major tasks to be done.

2. **Some prioritizing of tasks.** It helps to put a star beside the one task that must be accomplished that day. It may be a telephone call, information needed, a book to be checked out of the library, an appointment to be made, or a meeting to attend. While it may not be the most important task that day, it is the most imperative task.

   There are several systems for prioritizing lists of daily tasks. It does not matter what system you use, as long as it makes sense to you. Some hints on prioritizing follow this section.

3. **Flexibility.** Try not to have so many things on your list that the least little thing can throw your whole schedule off. Allow for tasks taking longer than anticipated, crises, and unexpected developments.

It is best to do your daily planning either first thing in the morning or just before going to bed. Whenever you choose to plan, make it a part of your daily schedule. Plan at the same time each day.

Remember, if you do not plan for something you want, you're unlikely to get it.

Setting Priorities. There are times when it is difficult to set priorities because everything we have to do that day is important or even urgent. Or perhaps nothing seems particularly important. In these instances there are two processes that may be helpful.

1. You can categorize your tasks and set priorities for them.

2. You can tap into your awareness to accomplish the same tasks.

To categorize and prioritize tasks, look at your entire list for the day. Put a 1 or a star by all the tasks that are *urgent*—that is, must be done that day. Hopefully, you will have only one urgent task. However, if you have more than one, there may be a logical order for the tasks. If so, it becomes easier to decide which to do first. Label them 1a, 1b, and so on. Whatever else you have to do that day, these tasks will get done.

Label *semi-urgent and important* tasks 2a, 2b, and so on, in the same way. These are tasks that are important but may not have to be accomplished that day. It may be necessary to work on them, but it is not necessary to finish. These tasks usually require some thought as well as actions. Give them the attention they need.

Label *important* tasks 3a, 3b, and so on. These are tasks that are significant but do not have a sense of urgency. You do not want to delay working on them; but if you have to choose what to work on, these tasks should come after urgent and semi-urgent tasks.

It is not necessary to label the last two categories of tasks, because you usually can choose to do or not do them. These are the tasks we categorize as *busy work* and *wasted time*. You determine what tasks fall into these categories; they may be different for each individual.

The second process of prioritizing involves simply looking at the entire list of things to do and allowing the priorities to emerge. You do not analyze them in a cognitive way but, rather, in an intuitive way. This will accomplish the setting of priorities in a different way from consciously analyzing and categorizing tasks.

One final word on setting priorities. Sometimes our individual priorities are not congruent with the demands of the situation, and it may be necessary to switch and adhere to other priorities. Do not fret; if it must be done, you waste more time and energy fretting than you would if you just went ahead and did it. You can get back to your priorities; they will not disappear.

EXERCISE 11.3. MY WORK PLAN

Objectives: To schedule high-energy tasks around personal high-energy periods; to become aware of one's own energy cycle; to develop strategies for coping when tasks and energy levels clash

Materials: A copy of Handout 11.3 and a pen or pencil for each participant; a schedule for a week, enlarged and posted where everyone can see it. The schedule should have all seven days and the hours from 5 A.M. through midnight.

Time: 30 to 45 minutes

Age/Education: 8th grade reading level and above

Number of Participants: 35

Preparation: Determine the usual working time frame for participants; develop the schedule and form for the chart based on those hours. For example, nurses working the late shift may have a working time of 10 P.M. to 6 A.M. Homemaker volunteers for an agency may have a working time of 10 A.M. to 2 P.M. While the schedule includes time before and after working time, the list of general activities and other times are built around working time.

Once the intended audience is known, you can generate a list of major activities for the group. Another way to do this is to consult with someone who works in the area on usual tasks and those that present the most time management problems. The most effective way of generating the list is to survey the participants.

Procedure: Form small groups of five to seven members distributed around tables in the same room. Introduce the exercise by telling participants that we all have energy cycles and will find it easier to accomplish some tasks if we schedule them around those energy periods. Ask participants to reflect on when they find it easiest to do their most difficult tasks.

Using the posted schedule for a week, show participants some examples of high-energy periods, such as the following:

- **Early morning:** Early morning people have no trouble waking up; they can move rapidly, talk, jog, and so on.

- **Late morning:** Some people just drift through the morning; they do not want to talk or be faced with problems before 10 A.M.; they can function, but they do not want to.

- **Early afternoon:** This is the low period for early morning people; some people actually function best during this time.

- **Late afternoon:** This usually is a rebounding time for early morning people. Late morning people begin to feel tired. Those who work 8 A.M. to 5 P.M. may find they are just getting into the swing about two hours before quitting time.

- **Early and late evening:** All of the above categories begin to wind down. People who become energized during this period can accomplish much.

There also are individuals whose energy levels fluctuate over a period of days but remain constant during a single day. For example:

- **Early week:** These individuals can get a lot accomplished on Monday and Tuesday but are less energetic by Thursday and all but wiped out by Friday.

- **Mid-week:** These individuals are somewhat slow to get into the job at the beginning of the week. However, by Wednesday their energy level has risen and they can get a lot done.

- **Late week:** These individuals have their highest energy levels when the usual work week is ending or has ended.

After describing these energy cycles, ask participants to fill out Handout 11.3. Allow 15 minutes for them to do so, then have them share in small groups.

Processing: Focus processing on new awareness. What emerged for participants that was new? What did they remember about their energy cycles? What changes could they make to better match energy levels and tasks?

My Work Plan

Directions: List the categories for your major activities during the day. Indicate what time of day you have the most energy for each activity, and/or the best day for each activity. List when each usually occurs.

General Activity	Best Time of Day	Best Day	Usually Occurs (Day)	Usually Occurs (Time)
1. Planning				
2. Thinking				
3. Writing				
4. Telephone				
5. Meetings				
6.				
7.				
8.				

Time of Day: Early morning, Late morning, Early afternoon, Late afternoon

Day: Early in week (Monday or Tuesday), Midweek (Wednesday), Late in week (Thursday or Friday), Weekends

Possible changes: _____

_____

_____

_____

_____

Handout 11.3. My Work Plan. *Permission is granted to photocopy for group use.*

EXERCISE 11.4. RECONSTRUCTING A DAY

Objectives: To increase awareness of the variety of feelings and moods experienced in a day; to focus on activities and their associated feelings, especially where possibilities for changes exist; to increase awareness of positive aspects of a day

Materials: Copies of Handouts 11.4A and 11.4B for each participant; pens or pencils; large sheets of newsprint; markers; masking tape for each small group

Time: 30 to 45 minutes

Age/Education: 8th grade reading level and above

Number of Participants: 35

Preparation: Prepare three sheets of newsprint for each small group titled Morning, Afternoon, and Evening, with subcategories of Feelings/ Moods, Activities-Positive, Activities-Negative.

Procedure: Divide the group into small groups and ask each group to sit around a table. All groups should remain in the same room. Introduce the exercise by asking participants to get comfortable and to put down anything they may be holding. Tell them they will try to reconstruct the previous day. If it is helpful, they can close their eyes. Read the directions on Handout 11.4A. Give examples and elaborations: For example, you could say after the first sentence, "There were many activities during your day, many feelings, many moods. You may have felt happy, rushed, frustrated, pleased, or satisfied. Try and recall all that transpired yesterday."

After reading the directions, instruct participants to complete the form with as much detail a possible. After forms are completed, allow time for small group discussion.

Processing: Distribute the prepared sheets of newsprint to each group. Within their groups, members are to list the primary feelings they experienced during the three periods. They also should list the kind of activities that produced the most positive and the most negative feelings. Kind of activity refers to categories such as commuting, socializing, or cleaning.

After the small groups have completed the lists, post them where on the wall and ask participants if they look for similarities and to identify differences. This is also an opportunity for participants to share suggestions for resolving some difficulties, for example, what to do when stuck in traffic to avoid frustration.

A further step, if time permits, is to ask participants how they perceive their day after the exercise, if their perception has changed. Some participants will become more aware of how they have focused on the negative aspects and ignored many positive aspects.

Distribute Handout 11.4B for participants to take home.

Reconstructing a Day

Directions: Reflect on your previous day, from the time you woke up to the time you went to sleep. Try to recall the events and movements of the day as they occurred. Recapture the moods and feelings you experienced during the morning, afternoon, and evening.

Period	Major Activities	Feelings/Mood
6 A.M.	_____	_____
7 A.M.	_____	_____
8 A.M.	_____	_____
9 A.M.	_____	_____
10 A.M.	_____	_____
11 A.M.	_____	_____
12 noon	_____	_____
1 P.M.	_____	_____
2 P.M.	_____	_____
3 P.M.	_____	_____
4 P.M.	_____	_____
5 P.M.	_____	_____
6 P.M.	_____	_____
7 P.M.	_____	_____
8 P.M.	_____	_____
9 P.M.	_____	_____
10 P.M.	_____	_____
11 P.M.	_____	_____
midnight	_____	_____

Handout 11.4A. Reconstructing a Day. *Permission is granted to photocopy for group use.*

Categories of Time Use

Important and Urgent: Tasks that must be done either immediately or in the near future are important and urgent. These tasks are not usually a time management problem. An example would be setting up a meeting to consider an unanticipated problem.

Important but Not Urgent: Attention to this category is what divides effective individuals from ineffective ones.

Most of the important things in life are not urgent but should be at the top of our tasks lists. If your activities are keyed to other people's priorities or to system-imposed deadlines that make things "urgent," you will never get around to your own priorities. An example might be a major written report or presentation.

Urgent but Not Important: In this category are those things that clamor for immediate action, but that we would assign a low priority if we examined them objectively. An example might be a request for information from someone.

Busy Work: These are tasks that are marginally worth doing but are not urgent or important. They are diversionary: They provide a feeling of activity and accomplishment while giving us an excuse to put off tackling those important but not urgent tasks, which have far greater benefit. Examples might include organizing and filing papers.

Wasted Time: The definition of wasted time is subjective. Use how you feel afterward as a criterion. If you feel uncomfortable, the task probably wasted time.

EXERCISE 11.5. ANALYSIS OF MY TASKS

Objectives: To help participants determine if they are spending most of their time on their most important tasks; to increase awareness of where they spend time and energy; to identify possible changes

Materials: Copies of Handouts 11.5A, 11.5B, 11.5C, and 11.5D for each participant; pens or pencils

Time: 60 to 90 minutes

Age/Education: 8th grade reading level and above

Number of Participants: This exercise can be done in a large or small group. It is more effective in a small group where participants have an opportunity to interact with others.

Preparation: Gather materials; reproduce Handouts 11.5A, 11.5B, 11.5C, and 11.5D; organize room.

Procedure: Distribute Handout 11.5A. Ask participants to list the five most important tasks related to the topic of the group. For example, if the workshop is for adolescents, the topic might be school-related tasks or their whole life tasks. After listing the most important tasks, participants should list their five most time-consuming tasks. If you are working with small groups, allow a short time for sharing in the groups.

Processing: Ask if there were any surprises in the lists—a show of hands for those whose lists were congruent, that is, the most time-consuming were also the most important. It is unusual to find congruence for most participants. They may want to discuss some of the reasons for incongruence.

The next step is to identify the time-consuming tasks, or parts of tasks, over which participants have some control. These are the tasks that hold promise for changes. To identify possible changes, ask group members to consider the following:

- **Eliminate:** Do not do the task; consider both the positive and the negative consequences of elimination.

- **Delegate:** Give the task or part of the task to someone else.

- **Ask for help:** You do not always have the authority do delegate. In these instances, there may be someone who can help with part or all of the task.

- **Find another way:** Review the task and see if there are other ways to accomplish it. Often, time-consuming tasks are the results of habits that can be modified or changed. For example, you might pay someone to cut the grass; buy pies for special occasions instead of baking them; equip every PC or workstation with access to central information sources; or communicate information via a newsletter or memo instead of holding meetings.

Have participants write down a specific action for change—for example, ask a son to cut the grass.

Distribute Handouts 11.5B, 11.5C, and 11.5D for participants to take home.

Analysis of My Tasks

Directions: List your most important tasks, in the order of their importance. The tasks can be work-related, family-related, or personal.

Most Important Tasks
(in order of importance)

1. _____

2. _____

3. _____

4. _____

5. _____

Now list your most time-consuming tasks.

Most Time-Consuming Tasks
(in order of time consumed)

1. _____

2. _____

3. _____

4. _____

5. _____

After compiling the lists, compare them to see if you are spending most of your time on those tasks that are most important.

Possible changes: _____

_____

Handout 11.5A. Analysis of My Tasks. *Permission is granted to photocopy for group use.*

Some Time Wasters Related to Time Management Functions

Planning Function

Takes time and thought to plan
Prefer to act or be spontaneous

Prioritizing Function

Confusion about relative importance of tasks
Shifting priorities
No clearly defined goals and objectives
Unable to distinguish between tasks

Deciding Function

Lack of confidence in self or information
Wanting *all* the facts before deciding
Fear of making a mistake
No decision-making process

Delegating Function

Lack of confidence in abilities and competencies of others
Assuming too much personal responsibility
Failure to set priorities
Not understanding how and when to delegate

Organizing Function

Operating by crises
Unrealistic time estimates
Responding to the urgent
Attempting too much
Problem orientation

Personal Competencies Function

Handling paper more than once
Inefficient reading habits
Lack of training
Overanxious
Refusal to delegate
Enjoyment of socializing
Inability to set priorities

Handout 11.5B. Some Time Wasters Related to Time Management Functions. *Permission is granted to photocopy for group use.*

Time Wasters and Management Functions

If you find you are engaged in the following	The failure of management may be
Having to meet unrealistic time estimates; no deadlines; managing crises; having numerous tasks to do at the same time; no daily plan; shifting priorities;	**Planning,** such as clear goals and objectives; priorities for tasks; communicated deadlines
Responding to multiple bosses; confused about responsibility and authority; duplication of effort	**Organizing,** such as a work plan with assigned tasks; agreed-upon priorities for tasks assigned to others; efficient workspace layout
Trying to do tasks for which you are not trained; unable to complete a task without interruptions, unless that is part of your job; missing time because of personal problems	**Staffing,** such as providing sufficient training and education; having sufficient staff; not being overstaffed; a process for helping workers cope with personal problems
Failure to cope with change; ongoing conflict; working alone when teamwork is called for; depressed motivation; uninteresting tasks; unimportant tasks; routine details	**Directing,** such as having a process to manage change; implementing conflict resolution skills; developing and supporting cooperation and teamwork; delegating important tasks; helping workers understand how what they do contributes to outcomes
Personal telephone calls many times of most days; chatting about personal topics constantly; visiting to or from others; not giving progress reports; being micro-managed; overcommitment because of an inability to say no; ineffective performance	**Controlling,** such as clear policies and expectations for conduct and performance; requesting progress reports; giving workers responsibility
Attending many meetings most days; having to ask for additional directions and clarifications; asking coworkers what is going on; constantly surprised by events; procrastinating; delaying or not making decisions	**Communicating,** such as giving clear directions for a task and checking to see if they were understood; keeping personnel up to date; involving personnel in making changes
Procrastinating; delaying by not making decisions	**Decision-Making,** such as understanding your decision-making style; knowing when you have sufficient facts to make a decision; knowing when to make decisions and when to involve others in the process

Handout 11.5C. Time Wasters and Management Functions. *Permission is granted to photocopy for group use.*

Strategies to Address Time Wasters

Function	Strategies
Planning	Recognize that planning saves time and concentrates energy on most important tasks; Emphasize results not activity; Set aside time for planning; Make "to do" lists
Prioritizing	Set clear, achievable goals and objectives; Prioritize "to do" lists; Work on most important tasks first; Shift priorities only when it is crucial to do so
Deciding	Develop a personal or team decision-making process; Decide to forgive yourself for making mistakes; Learn to make decisions without having to have all the facts; Develop a network of reliable information sources
Delegating	Delegate tasks and give resources necessary to accomplish the tasks; Set priorities daily and communicate them to others to whom tasks will be delegated; Learn how and when to delegate
Organizing	Learn to distinguish between categories of tasks; Set realistic time estimates; Do not procrastinate; Work on large tasks daily; Organize your work space; Make daily "to do" lists; Develop a problem prevention orientation; Have realistic expectations of yourself and others; Allow for shifts in priorities
Personal Competence	Develop a "do it now" attitude for handling paper; Try to handle each piece of paper only once; Learn and practice speed reading; Save socializing for after hours;Learn to say no; Concentrate on goals; Work on important tasks first; Group telephone calls; Save junk mail and magazines to go through once a week; Practice delegating

Handout 11.5D. Strategies to Address Time Wasters. *Permission is granted to photocopy for group use.*

Mini-Lecture: Paperwork

Paperwork can be divided into roughly four categories; correspondence, reports, forms, and records. While the paperwork faced by workers in various settings may differ in quantity, all workers must complete some paperwork.

Correspondence. Most workers, especially those in offices, will deal with correspondence. In fact, this is one task that can expand to fill entire days You must respond to letters from customers, suppliers, and clients, of course; but there are ways to do it more efficiently.

1. Write a response on the bottom of the incoming letter or memorandum, make a copy, and mail.

2. Do not spend time writing a rough draft; just type a final copy and mail it. Most software will correct spelling and punctuation errors. After you frame your reply, you should only have to sign the letter.

3. Do not write a reply at all; instead, call or visit the individual and transact the business over the telephone or in person.

4. Use preprinted forms on which you write your letter at the top and the bottom has space for a reply. These usually are on carbonless paper, which gives a copy without using either carbons or a copying machine.

5. Use dictating equipment. You can dictate letters in places or at times when you cannot write (e.g., in a car or on an airplane).

Reports. Many workers must write reports at least monthly; some must do so weekly or even daily. Below are some tips for making the task go quickly.

1. When you learn that you must submit a report, begin gathering materials and data immediately.

   a. Make a folder to hold all materials relating to the report.

   b. Put the due date in bold letters on the outside of the folder and in at least two places on your desk calendar; include a reminder one month before it is due and the date it is due.

2. Make sure you know the correct format for the report as well the information required. Put it in the folder.

3. Make an outline for the report. The outline can serve as your guide for collecting information and writing the report.

4. It may be useful to write a list of all bits and pieces of information you need for the report and staple it to the inside of the folder. That way, you can check off information as it is collected and have a reminder of what other information you need. You can then work on the report by gathering information each week, and you won't have to run around at the last minute trying to locate missing pieces.

5. The actual report writing can be done in one of two ways: a little at a time or all at once. Most people typically use one or the other, and do not feel comfortable switching. Those who write a little at a time will work on the report off and on for several weeks, and will not write the various sections in the order they appear in the report. Rather, they write the sections as they find the information for them. Then, when they are ready to put the report together, it's just a matter of putting it in order.

   Those individuals who write all at once must have all of the information collected before they can begin writing. They prefer to start at the beginning and keep writing until they are through. It is terribly frustrating for them not to have all of their information.

   Either method can be efficient and effective. The point is to avoid wasting time: gather your information and work on—not necessarily write—the report daily or weekly as you have time; *do not delay.* Procrastination is more time-consuming than writing.

Forms.   There are few careers in the United States today that do not require forms. There are also few forms that do not request unnecessary information. There are two primary time-saving procedures for forms: Handle them only once and review them to eliminate unnecessary items.

1. Handle it only once: After you have read the form and understand its purpose, fill it out right away. Do not file it, put it in a pile, or otherwise delay filling it out. Most forms do not require a great deal of time to complete, and if you are interrupted, you can get back to it easily.

2. If you have forms in your office, review them with an eye toward simplifying them. Eliminate items that request unnecessary information. Ask these questions of each and every item: Why do we need this piece of information? How would it hurt to eliminate this piece of information? Is this item redundant—for example, asking for both age and date of birth?

3. Locate software that could be used to fill out forms on the computer. This is especially helpful if there are numerous forms to be filled out that require much of the same information.

Records. Keeping records can be very time consuming, particularly if you have not developed a system that allows for quick and easy retrieval. After all, one of the most important requirements for a record keeping system is rapid access to needed information. thus, it is crucial that the system be developed to allow you to get documents in a timely manner.

The suggestions that follow are based on the assumptions that you are keeping personal records and do not need a system for keeping records for others, that it is important in your work that you have documentation, and that you have a need for paper copies. Electronic record keeping is separate topic; the focus here is on ways to handle paper.

1. Set up a system that makes sense to you. This will make it easier to retrieve needed information. One way to organize is by topic. That is, all documents relating to a particular topic are in one file. If this is a large file, you can have sub-topics files. For example, if the topic "department budget" is too large for just one file, sub-topics such as "department budget plan" and "budget by month" could be set up. In the particular file would be all documents, including memorandums, relating to that topic. Thus, when you need information, all of it would be in the single file.

2. Before filing a document, decide on its potential importance. Is it likely to be needed at some point in time? some materials have a high potential for future importance, such as a memo assigning you a specific task with a due date. Memories can be unreliable, and this memo is a record for you and others of the stated requirements and expectations. Other documents, such as announcements, may never be needed and do not need to be filed.

3. Develop a time line for keeping categories of documents. Some documents, such as contracts, you would want to keep a long time, while

something such as a time schedule for a completed project could be discarded. Discard documents that have little or no potential for being needed or used in the foreseeable future. After all, space usually is limited. The one exception to this suggestion is when a law or regulation mandates the length of time documents must be kept.

Mini-Lecture: Meetings

Here are some questions to ponder and answer.

1. When you chair a meeting, do you prepare an agenda and distribute it prior to the meeting?

2. Is the meeting time set by you at your convenience?

3. Do you try to wait until all or most of the participants are present before beginning the meeting, even if it means not starting on time?

4. Do you let the majority rule even if you disagree?

5. Do you hold regular meetings (e.g., once a week)?

Making Meetings Productive. When time management workshop members are asked to list their concerns, many list meetings as time wasters. Meetings are perceived as wasting time for many reasons:

- They are not focused; that is, they have unclear goals and objectives,

- They begin and end late.

- The method of decision making leaves some feeling discounted.

- Members are not consulted about the time of the meeting.

- Nothing of importance is discussed; the meeting is focused on trivia or irrelevant issues.

- A few people dominate the meeting.

Chairing Meetings. If you have the responsibility for chairing meetings, you can manage them so that your task is accomplished, relationships are enhanced, and time is well-spent. Whether it is a committee meeting or a staff meeting makes no difference; either can be conducted with efficiency.

As in all time management processes, planning is of the utmost importance. Time spent in planning ensures that the meeting is focused and participants feel a sense of accomplishment. Planning includes these steps:

1. **Set the agenda.** Solicit ideas and suggestions from participants whenever possible. Using these suggestions promotes a sense of involvement. If the task is pretty clear-cut, have the agenda reflect the primary topics to be discussed and decided.

2. **Distribute the agenda prior to the meeting.** It puts people at a disadvantage when they do not have the agenda or topics beforehand. Many participants are reluctant to making decisions under these conditions because they have not had time to reflect and feel comfortable in making a decision. They may need to gather information, consult with others, or just think things through before the meeting. It is not uncommon for participants to delay making decisions, necessitating another meeting.

3. **Distribute information pertinent to the agenda before the meeting.** If you want the discussion to be focused on the issues or decisions to be made at the meeting, make sure participants have related information prior to the meeting. Most people cannot read, listen, and talk at the same time.

4. **Consult about setting the meeting time.** As much as possible, allow participants some say in when the meeting will take place. It makes people feel you respect them and their work when you try to plan meetings around their best time. It is not always feasible to do this; however, the attempt should be made.

5. **Begin and end on time.** Nothing is more annoying than making an effort to attend a meeting on time only to have the chairperson delay the start waiting for someone else to get there. It makes those who made the effort to get there on time feel less important than the one who is late. It also conveys a lack of respect for the time of others.

6. **Make sure the meetings are time-bound.** Meetings should have a definite beginning and ending time. If the meeting is to be one hour in length, make sure you end it when approximately 60 minutes are up.

People appreciate being able to plan their activities, and meetings that run long can throw schedules off. It is always better to end early than to run over time.

7. **Time discussions.** When issues are to be discussed, set a time limit. You might say, for example, "We will allow 20 minutes for the discussion on merit salary increases." If it appears that this is insufficient time to allow everyone to have input, you can allow more time or table the issue until the next meeting. When discussions are protracted, more information, reflection, or consultation are needed. It becomes counterproductive to allow the discussion to continue. If it is unlikely that a satisfactory resolution can be reached, you should explore other alternatives: For example, you might assign a subcommittee to study the issue and provide information to the entire group; you might hold a special meeting to focus only on that issue; or you could generate a list of solutions to be discussed.

8. **Focus meetings.** Keep the discussion focused on the main topics; stick to the agenda as much as possible. Use your facilitation skills to keep the discussion focused and to make participants feel heard. Skills that help include reflection, summarizing, linking, and identification of primary issues or concerns. Do not allow extraneous questions, comments, or statements to deflect the discussion.

There are times when important events or issues emerge after the agenda has been set. You should be flexible enough to adjust to the new situation; but make sure the new issues are more important then the items on the agenda.

9. **Involve everyone.** As chair, you should solicit input and opinions from everyone, and you should make sure that everyone feels involved. Before accepting a decision, ask if anyone has a question or comment. You may find that the quiet individual has an important point that changes everything. Individuals who are not involved in the discussion and the decision may not feel committed to implementing the decision.

10. **Take minutes.** If there is a secretary responsible for recording the minutes, make sure he or she notes *what* was done: That is, the important points made, issues raised, and all decisions should be in the minutes, not who said what, who made or seconded motions, and so on. The minutes should be distributed to all participants.

If there is no secretary, the chairperson or a designated individual should make notes on the decisions made and important issues or concerns raised. These should be approximately one page in length, typed, and distributed to all attendees, with the understanding that they can be corrected if in error. You will find that it saves time if what was said is in writing rather than in an individual's memory. Avoid hurt feelings and misunderstandings by distributing minutes and listing attendees in alphabetical order. Any time a list of names appears on anything, order the list alphabetically, regardless of the status of the individuals.

Participating in Meetings. As a participant, you can help to make meetings productive and not time-wasters. Although you cannot do many of the things noted above, there are several other things you can do.

1. If an agenda has not been set or distributed, ask for one. Make it a request, not a demand, and put it on the basis of being helpful to all the participants.

2. Once you know the topics on the agenda, prepare for the meeting. Do not wait for information to be disseminated; it may not be. Seek information and *read it* before attending the meeting.

3. Make a list or note any points that you want clarified. It may be useful to note any points you want to make.

4. Arrive on time and be ready to begin. Do not let socializing interfere with the meeting. If the chairperson does not begin on time, request that the meeting start. Sometimes, all it takes is a reminder.

5. Keep your input focused on the topics at hand.

6. Use your facilitation skills: reflection, linking, clarifying, and questioning.

7. Be concrete; do not waffle or be ambiguous.

8. Be assertive, not aggressive or apathetic.

Tools for Time Management

1. **Set goals** (objectives) and establish priorities, and work on them daily.

2. **Plan.** Nothing is more important!

3. **Schedule your time.** Recognize and accept that there is some time over which you have no control.

4. **Reschedule your time.** Your schedule will be interrupted continually. People will have needs that must be met now. Work out ways to reschedule things you have been forced to postpone.

5. **Write it down!** Don't trust to your memory; if something is important, put it in writing.

6. **Have follow-up systems.** Being accountable and holding others accountable are great time savers and help eliminate procrastination.

7. **Delegate.** Do only what you can do best and delegate whatever you can; but don't delegate your job, that which you are supposed to do or only you can do.

8. **Use different reading techniques for different material:** scan, speed read, study, analyze.

9. **Assume interruptions.** Don't make your schedule too tight; set aside time to return calls and to see people.

10. **Communicate.** Nothing wastes time more than misunderstandings. Be clear and concise; get feedback; and establish regular information flow systems.

Handout 11.6A. Tools for Time Management. *Permission is granted to photocopy for group use.*

Some Basic Time Management Strategies

Planning

Plan each day and try to plan at the same time each day.
Make a daily "to do" list.
Prioritize the list and work on the most important items first.
Set life goals and objectives, and work to achieve them.

Organizing

Schedule your tasks.
Plan for interruptions. Don't schedule too tightly.
Plan ahead for recurring tasks, such as meals.
Organize materials *before you need them* (e.g., pack the night before a trip).
Anticipate delays.
Delegate wherever possible and feasible.

Controlling

Distinguish between tasks that are urgent and important and those that are just urgent.
When needed, eliminate all tasks that are not urgent and important.
Practice a "do it now" attitude. The price of procrastination may be too high.
Ask yourself this question frequently: *What is the best use of my time at this moment?* Act on the answer.

Directing

For any 10- to 15-minute period, ask yourself this: *What can be done?* Here are some possible answers:
    Go through a pile of papers on the desk and sort
       and throw some away
    Clear the desk
    Return a call
    Request needed information
    Dust a room
    Read a page, a paragraph, a, article, or a brochure
    Plan a task into its components
    Work on a piece of a larger task
    Make an appointment

Handout 11.6B. Some Basic Time Management Strategies. *Permission is granted to photocopy for group use.*

Chapter 12

SELF-HELP AND SUPPORT GROUPS

Self-help and support groups have many similarities and tend to be closer to counseling or therapy groups than other types of psychoeducational groups. The subject matter is more sensitive, members deal with basic issues as well as current crises, and feelings are emphasized more than cognitions. These groups may not have a professional leader, although professionals are used to some extent. The leader of a self-help or support group may need to have preparation in group counseling to be most effective, even though much of the work is psychoeducational in nature.

Corey (1995) distinguished between self-help and support groups by noting first that the terms are often used interchangeably and that the origin of the group determines the category. He suggested that support groups usually are developed by a professional helping organization or individual, while self-help groups tend to emphasize the independence and responsibility of members to help themselves. For purposes of the discussion here, I make no distinction between them. The term used will be self-help, but this includes support groups.

DISTINCTIVE CHARACTERISTICS

Gladding (1995) proposed the following distinctive characteristics of self-help groups:

- mutual assistance;

- peer leadership;

- member-determined directions, goal, and purpose;

- emphasis on similarities of members around a common concern;

- interaction with other members who have similar conditions and have benefited;

- an underlying theme that unites members; and

- support for accomplishing personal goals.

Self-help groups differ from other kind of groups on these characteristics in level and intensity. They are less leader-directed and more member-directed, but there is a need for the trained group leader.

Mutual Assistance

Members are expected to help one another. A basic premise for self-help groups is that each member has something to contribute to the group and to other members. Assistance is two-way, and all members are expected to give and to receive.

Peer Leadership

The responsibility for the functioning of the group is distributed among members and the leader. Some groups do not have a consistent leader, but rely on each member to assume leadership in turn. The emphasis is on self-help with less reliance on the professional.

Member-Determined Direction, Goals, and Purposes

All goals and purposes are decided by members in self-help groups. The leader can provide suggestions and implement strategies to achieve the goals, but members are in charge of the direction for the group. There are few, if any, leader-imposed objectives.

Common Concerns and Similarities

Members maintain their uniqueness while searching for similarities. The emphasis is on similarities around a common concern. As in any group, situations and individuals differ, but similarities tend to be more easily discernible in self-help groups, and members begin to look for these similarities from the first session.

Interactions with Members Who Model

It seems to be therapeutic for members to actively interact with other members who have benefited from being in the group and dealing with the problem or concern. Seeing others who have been in similar circumstances and hearing how they coped or dealt with the situation promotes hope and provides encouragement.

Underlying Themes

Universality is a therapeutic factor and appears to be strong in self-help groups. There is a conscious search for common underlying themes to unite members. A kind of "we are all in this together" attitude reduces isolation and helps form supportive connections.

Support for Personal Goals

The self-help group allows members to try new behaviors and skills, encourages them, cheers them if they are successful, and supports them if they are not. This support encourages members to continue trying, modifying, and changing until they are successful. Members learn that goal setting and achievement is an ongoing process and that failure is not the worst thing that can happen— giving up is.

PRIMARY FOCUS

There are several kinds of self-help groups, but most can be categorized as dealing with one of the following; psychological problems such as depression; medical illnesses such as cancer; life circumstances such as divorce; or life crises such as death. These groups are characterized as having less of a here-and-now focus and as valuing interpersonal honesty, exploration, confrontation, self-disclosure, and emotional expression. There is considerable information exchange and learning, which helps these groups bridge counseling or therapy with a psychoeducational aspect. A lot of time and effort is spent helping members learn about the condition, circumstance, or situation.

MAIN GOALS

The main goals for self-help groups are these:

- To empower and encourage members to obtain control over and improve the quality of their lives, relationships, and self-acceptance.

- To provide an emotional support system that decreases alienation and isolation, moderates despair, and increases hopefulness and personal responsibility.

- To help members derive a greater sense of joy and satisfaction from life as it is with all of its barriers, constraints, setbacks, and disappointments.

- To practice and learn new ways of behaving and relating.

LEADER RESPONSIBILITIES

A professional leader of a psychoeducational self-help group has somewhat different responsibilities than the leader of other types of psychoeducational groups. Since the direction, goals, and purpose for the group are member-determined, you must solicit input and clarify goals and intent. You can then develop strategies to implement the objectives and goals, but these may also have to be approved by members.

Another responsibility is to learn about the condition or to locate other professionals who can provide members with needed information. You must decide how you will impart this information as well, and should follow guidelines in chapter 2. You need to know enough about the condition to facilitate groups even when the in-depth knowledge comes from an outsider who will probably attend only one or two meetings.

You may find it difficult to be both a member and a leader and to empower members to take charge of the group. A basic premise is that members assume responsibility for self-care, which means a decreased reliance on authorities, such as group leaders.

Guidelines for Structuring Learning

The following guidelines have been adapted from those presented by Stern, Lawrence, and Duluy (1992) for groups of medically ill patients. The psychoeducational component has been extracted and modified for other types of self-help groups that are homogeneous and designed to be relatively short-term (that is, 20 or fewer sessions).

The primary guidelines are to emphasize education and therapeutic alternatives, teach members how to relieve anxiety and stress, identify needed lifestyle changes and teach behavioral steps to achieve these changes, and emotional support.

Emphasize Education. Members probably do not have sufficient and accurate information about their conditions. They may not have encountered the circumstance before, and have no idea what are expected behaviors or feelings. If they are dealing with an acute or chronic illness, they may have little knowledge about the etiological factors, expected treatment, or potential outcomes. If the group members are family members of someone who is ill, they need this information so as to best care for and react to the illness. The leader should obtain reading materials and a list of questions about the condition; talk with a professional about optimum treatment, as well as about what the individual can do to help him- or herself; and secure the services of someone to teach a session on these topics.

Anxiety and Stress. Anxiety and stress often contribute to the condition, illness, or circumstance. Stress reduces immunity, thereby giving rise to infections; can increase blood pressure and constriction of the arteries; and increases muscle tension, leading to pain, such as lower back pain and headaches. Relaxation moderates reactions to stress, reduces anxiety, and allows the individual to feel more in control. The sample psychoeducational self-help group in this chapter focuses on stress reduction.

Changes in Lifestyle. Teaching members the benefits of changes in diet, exercise, work habits, and use of leisure is another task for the leader. Understanding the effects of their present lifestyle and setting reasonable goals for changes can improve their attitudes as well as their physical health. A leader needs to be knowledgeable in these areas.

Emotional Expression.   Self-help groups are developed around a problem, condition, or concern: Something is awry or wrong. Whatever the situation, intense feelings usually are aroused. These feelings can be openly expressed and dealt with in self-help groups. Facilitating expression of feelings is a primary goal for these groups.

Risk Factors

There are conditions, characteristics, and events that contribute to increased potential for stress when we are faced with a life condition over which we have little or no control. These risk factors range from manageable to unmanageable, and differ in their extent and intensity: That is, you may be able to tolerate more of a particular factor than others, or you may be prone to responding to even a slight presence of a factor where others can accept and deal with more of the same factor.

The factors associated with increased potential for uncomfortable stress are categorized as existential, work-related, stress management skills, negative stress management behaviors, personal characteristics, and uncontrollable events. Examples of each are provided in Table 12. 1.

Following is a series of exercises designed to address some of these risk factors. They can be used together, in sequence, or each can stand alone.

TABLE 12.1
Risk Factors

Categories	Examples
Existential/Spiritual	Lack of purpose in life Unclear, unattainable goals Conflicting values Confused beliefs
Work-Related	Boring tasks Conflict with coworkers Conflict with boss External pressure to "do more," succeed, etc. Ambiguous or uncertain environment Responsibility without authorization Inadequate resources to get the job done (e.g., time, equipment, personnel) Feeling unappreciated or devalued Confused lines of authority Multiple bosses
Inadequate Stress Management Skills	Rigidity versus flexibility in attitude Refusal to change or seek new ways to cope Neglecting emotional support systems Poor health management and habits; neglect (e.g., lack of exercise, eating on the run)
Negative Stress Management Behaviors	Alcohol abuse Drug abuse Overeating Undereating Frequent temper tantrums
Personal Characteristics	Need for perfectionism Pessimistic in outlook Sense of overresponsibility for other's well-being Suppressing, denying, or repressing emotions
Uncontrolled or Uncontrollable Events	The economy Bad weather (e.g., hurricanes) Taxes Accidents Death Severe or chronic illness

EXERCISE 12.1. MY EXISTENTIAL/SPIRITUAL SELF

Objectives: To increase awareness of personal involvement with existential/spiritual issues; to identify existential/spiritual strengths

Materials: A sheet of paper with a large circle drawn on it for each member; markers or pencils; glue sticks; masking tape; magazines or catalogs; copies of Handout 12.1, which lists the following categories:

- lack of purpose in life,

- encounter(s) with death,

- present conflicts in values,

- a few awe-inspiring experiences,

- present status of religious beliefs,

- extent of major commitments,

- difficult choices being faced, and

- presently held doubts.

Time: 60 to 90 minutes

Age/Education: Adults of 6th grade reading level and above

Number of Participants: Works best with a small group with 10 or fewer members but can be used with a larger group of 20 to 25.

Preparation: Gather materials; reproduce Handout 12.1.

Procedure: Explain the focus for this exercise—existential/spiritual issues. Include these points: Healthy people realize that there is a continuing search for truth and purpose in life; know that values that must be examined; commit to causes and services; seek hope and meaning; experience despair; define faith as acceptance of the unknown and unknowable.

For some, religion is the source of spirituality. This exercise puts their spiritual life in focus and identifies potential spiritual concerns that may contribute to stress as well as strengths that can be used.

Pass out materials and explain to members that they are to write words or phrases associated with each of the categories on Handout 12.1. Next, they are to place symbols for each of the categories in the circle, forming a seal. (See Figure 12.1 for an example.) They are free to draw the symbols or to find pictures in the magazines and catalogs that symbolize the categories.

Allow 20 to 30 minutes for completion of the seals. Depending on the time available, sharing of the seals can be done in the entire group or in small groups. Seals can be posted on the wall with masking tape. Allow enough time for each person to describe his or her seal.

Processing: The focus for processing emphasizes unused spiritual resources. Ask if any surprises emerged, new awarenesses, remembered satisfactions, or directions for the future. Members can write their answers down so they can refer back to them. Writing also ensures that each member has an opportunity to make associations.

Figure 12.1. Example of an individual seal.

Existential/Spiritual Risk Factors

Lack of purpose in life:

Encounter(s) with death:

Present conflicts in values:

A few awe-inspiring experiences:

Present status of religious beliefs:

Extent of major commitments:

Difficult choices being faced:

Presently held doubts:

Handout 12.1. Existential/Spiritual Risk Factors. *Permission is granted to photocopy for group use.*

EXERCISE 12.2. DEMANDS AND REWARDS

Objectives: To increase awareness of demands or requirements placed on you and another person in a work relationship; to make explicit your expectations/needs/desires for rewards from this person; to develop an awareness of the other's expectations/needs/desires for rewards from you; to assess the stress factor

Materials: Pencil or pen for each member; one or two sheets of paper for each member

Time: 60 to 90 minutes

Age/Education: Adults of 9th grade reading level and above

Number of Participants: 20 to 25

Preparation: Gather materials.

Procedure: Introduce the exercise by telling members the objectives for the exercise. Ask them to select one work relationship with which to work. This may be a relationship that is satisfying or one that is troublesome. A neutral or indifferent relationship will not produce much awareness or learning. Ask participants to write the person's name or work role at the top of the page: Work roles include boss, secretary, and coworker. Ask members to write their responses to the following questions. Allow time for them to write down their responses.

1. Write all words or phrases that come to mind when you think of this person.

2. List the person's negative traits or qualities.

3. List his or her positive qualities.

4. Identify demands or requirements this person places on or expects from you.

5. Label the items in #4 **E** if the demand or requirement is explicit, and **I** if it is implicit.

6. Identify demands or requirements you expect of this person.

7. In #6, label the items **E** if explicit, and **I** if implicit.

8. List the rewards you expect from the person and estimate the percentage of time you receive each.

9. Review what you have written and write a paragraph describing the stress you experience in the relationship due to the other person's implicit demands and requirements.

Processing: Help members identify implicit demands and encourage them to formulate steps to make these explicit, *if the reward would be worth the effort*. Members can be encouraged to decide how they can let go of unrewarding demands or behavior, thereby reducing stress.

EXERCISE 12.3. EMOTIONAL RISK FACTORS

Objectives: To increase awareness of the wide variety of feelings experienced; to identify major blocks to feeling expressions; to enhance expression and awareness of pleasant feelings

Materials: A sheet of paper with a circle drawn on it for each participant; crayons, felt-tip markers, or oil pastels in sufficient number so that each member has access to a variety of colors; a blank sheet of paper for each member; pens or pencils

Time: 60 to 90 minutes

Age/Education: 4th grade reading level and above

Number of Participants: 20 to 25

Preparation: Gather materials; organize room.

Procedure: Introduce the exercise by telling members that healthy people feel deeply, are sensitive to feelings in themselves and in others, are able to experience a wide range of feelings, and are able to access their feelings easily. Sometimes even healthy people try to block or deny unpleasant feelings, cannot find words to express their feelings, confuse experiencing a feeling with acting on it, or become so mired in a feeling that they block off other feelings.

Distribute the blank sheet of paper and pens and ask participants to mentally divide the sheet into four sections. In the upper left section (#1), ask them to list all unpleasant feeling they experienced in the previous week. Allow time for them to construct their lists. In the upper right section (#2), ask them to list all pleasant feelings they experienced in the same time period. After both lists are completed, have them put the sheet aside.

Distribute the paper with a circle and markers. Ask members to examine their lists of feelings and to select a color for each. They are to use the color to fill in the circle in the shape and to the extent they experienced the feeling. For example, if sadness was the strongest and most persistent feeling, they could use a dark blue or grey to color in a large cloud shape in the circle. Members should look at both lists and make choices before beginning to fill in the circle.

When the circles are finished, have members show theirs and describe what feelings the colors illustrate.

Return to the sheet with the lists. In the lower right section (#3) have members list steps they can take to decrease the level and frequency of the unpleasant feelings. In the lower right section (#4) have members list what they can do to increase the level and frequency of pleasant feelings.

Processing: Allow time for sharing and focus processing on awareness that has emerged during the exercise.

REFERENCES

Association for Specialists in Group Work. (1990). *Ethical guidelines for group counselors and professional standards for the training of group workers.* Alexandria, VA: Author.

Association for Specialists in Group Work. (1991). *Ethical guidelines for group counselors.* Alexandria, VA: Author.

Bandura, A. (1977). *Social learning theory.* Englewood Cliffs, NJ: Prentice-Hall.

Benjamin, A. (1987). *The helping interview.* Boston: Houghton Mifflin.

Berenson, B. G., Mitchell, K. M., & Laney, R. C. (1968). Therapeutic conditions after therapist-initiated confrontation. *Journal of Clinical Psychology, 24,* 363-364.

Bion, W. (1961). *Experiences in groups and other papers.* London: Tavistock.

Bloom, B. S., Krathwohl, D. R., & Masia, B. B. (1956). *Taxonomy of educational objectives: Handbook 1—Cognitive domain.* New York: David McKay.

Campbell, D. (1974). *If you don't know where you are going, you'll probably end up somewhere else.* Niles, IL: Argus Communications.

Corey, G. (1995). *Theory and practice of counseling and psychotherapy* (5th ed.). Pacific Grove, CA: Brooks/Cole.

Devine, E. C. (1992). Effects of psychoeducational care for adult surgical patients: A meta-analysis of 191 studies. *Patient Education and Counseling, 19*(2), 129-142.

Dollard, J., & Miller, N. E. (1950). *Personality and psychotherapy.* New York: McGraw-Hill.

Douglas, M., & Mueser, K. T. (1990). Teaching conflict resolution skills to the chronically mental ill: Social skills training groups for briefly hospitalized patients. *Behavior Modification, 124*(4), 519-547.

Durlak, J. A., Fuhrman, T., & Lampman, C. (1991). Effectiveness of cognitive-behavior therapy for maladapting children: A meta-analysis. *Psychological Bulletin, 110*, 204-214.

Egan, G. (1975). *Exercises in helping skills.* Pacific Grove, CA: Brooks/Cole.

Fawzy, I., & Fawzy, N. W. (1994). A structured psychoeducational intervention for cancer patients. *General Hospital Psychiatry, 16*(3), 149-192.

Fawzy, I., Fawzy, N. W., Aront, L. A., & Pasnau, R. O. (1995). Critical review of psychosocial interventions in cancer care. *Archives of General Psychiatry, 52*(2), 100-113.

Fiedler, F. (1978). Recent developments in research on the contingency model. In L. Berkowitz (Ed.), *Group process* (pp. 62-78). New York: Academic Press.

Fine, S., Forth, A., Gilbert, M., & Haley, G. (1991). Group therapy for adolescent depressive disorder: Comparison of social skills and therapeutic support. *Journal of the American Academy of Child and Adolescent Psychiatry, 30*, 79-85.

Forester, B., Cornfield, D. S., Fleiss, J. L., & Thomas, S. (1993). Group psychotherapy during radiotherapy. *American Journal of Psychiatry, 150*(11), 1700-1706.

Gagné, R. M. (1965). The analysis of instructional objectives for the design of instruction. In R. Glaser (Ed.), *Teaching machines and programmed learning II: Data and directions.* Washington, DC: Department of Audio-Visual Instruction, National Education Association.

Gamble, E. H., Elder, S., & Lashley, J. K. (1989). Group behavior therapy: A selective review of the literature. *Medical Psychotherapy: An International Journal, 2*, 193-204.

Garrison, K. D., & Magoon, R. A. (1972). *Educational psychology.* Columbus, OH: Charles E. Merrill.

Gladding, S. (1995). *Group work: A counseling specialty* (2nd ed.). Englewood Cliffs, NJ: Prentice-Hall.

Goldstein, A. P., & Glick, B. (1987). Aggression replacement training. *Journal of Counseling and Development, 65,* 356-367.

Gough, H. (1975). *Manual for the California Psychological Inventory.* Palo Alto, CA: Consulting Psychologist Press.

Hall, D., & Cockburn, E. (1990). Developing management skills. *Management Education and Development, 21*(1), 41-50.

Hershey, P., & Blanchard, K. (1977). *Management of organizational behavior: Utilizing human resources* (3rd ed.). Englewood Cliffs, NJ: Prentice-Hall.

Holland, J. (1973). *Making vocational choices: A theory of careers.* Englewood Cliffs, NJ: Prentice Hall.

Hull, C. L. (1943). *Principles of behavior.* New York: Appleton-Century-Croft.

James, W. (1890). *The principles of psychology.* New York: Holt, Rinehart & Winston.

Judd, C. H. (1908). The relation of special training to general intelligence. *Educational Review, 36,* 36-37.

Kamps, D. M., Leonard, B. R., Vernon, S., & Dugan, E. P. (1992, Summer). Teaching social skills to students with autism to increase peer interactions in an integrated first-grade classroom. *Journal of Applied Behavior Analysis, 29*(2), 281-288.

Khattri, N. (1991). *An assessment of the social validity of cooperative learning and conflict resolution programs in an alternative inner city high school.* New York: Columbia University.

Kuder, F. (1963, 1987). *Kuder General Interest Survey.* Chicago, IL: Science Research Associates.

Kurtz, R. R., & Jones, J. E. (1973). Confrontation: Types, conditions, and outcomes. In J. W. Pfeiffer & J. E. Jones (Eds.), *The 1973 annual handbook for group facilitators.* LaJolla, CA: University Associates Publishers.

la Salivia, T. A. (1993). Enhancing addictions treatment through psychoeducational groups. *Journal of Substance Abuse Treatment, 10*(5), 439-444.

Maslow, A. (1943). A theory of human motivation. *Psychological Review, 50,* 370-396.

Moreau, A. S. (1994). Improvising social skills of third grade students through conflict resolution training. *ERIC,* ED 375. 33 4.

Mowrer, O. M. (1960). *Learning theory and behavior.* New York: John Wiley.

Murray, H. (1938). *Explorations in personality.* New York: Oxford University Press.

Newstrom, J., & Scannell, E. (1991). *Still more games trainers play.* New York: McGraw-Hill.

Pavlov, I. (1927). *Conditioned reflexes.* New York: Oxford University Press.

Rotter, J. B. (1959). Substituting good behavior for bad. *Contemporary Psychology, 4,* 176-178.

Shure, M. B. (1993, December). I can problem solve: Interpersonal cognitive problem solving for your children. *Early Childhood Development and Care,* 49-64.

Skinner, B. F. (1953). *Science and human behavior.* New York: Macmillan.

Stein, C. H., Cislo, D. A., & Ward, M. (1994, July 18). Collaboration in the college classroom: Evaluation of a social network and social skills program for undergraduates and people with serious mental illnesses. *Psychosocial Rehabilitation Journal,* (1), 13-33.

Stern, M., Lawrence, M., & Duluy, J. (1992, October). *Groups for the medically ill.* Paper presented at the Mid-Atlantic Group Psychotherapy Society Conference, Williamsburg, VA.

Swell, L. (1992). Education for success: A program to enhance the self-concept of freshmen on a large college campus—An evaluation. *Canadian Journal of Higher Education, 22*(2), 68-72.

Thorndike, E. L. (1913). *Educational psychology.* New York: Columbia University Press.

Walton, R. (1987). *Managing conflict.* Reading, MA: Addison-Wesley.

Weist, M. D., Vannatta, K., & Wayland, K. (1993). Social skills training for abused girls: Interpersonal skills training for sexually abused girls. *Behavior Change, 10*(4), 244-252.

Wertheimer, M. (1959). *Productive thinking* (2nd ed.). New York: Harper & Row.

Wolpe, J. (1958). *Psychotherapy by reciprocal inhibition.* Palo Alto, CA: Stanford University Press.

Worchel, S., & Shebilske, W. (1992). *Psychology principles and applications* (4th ed.). Englewood Cliffs, NJ: Prentice Hall.

Yalom, I. (1985). *The theory and practice of group psychotherapy* (3rd ed.). New York: Basic Books.

Yalom, I. (1995). *The theory and practice of group psychotherapy* (4th ed.). New York: Basic Books.

BIBLIOGRAPHY

Berenson, B., & Carkhuff, R. (1967). *Beyond counseling and psychotherapy.* New York: Holt, Rinehart & Winston.

Caserta, M. S., & Land, D. A. (1993). Intrapersonal resources and the effectiveness of self-help groups for bereaved older adults. *Gerontologist, 33*(5), 619-629.

Hitch, P. J., Fielding, R. G., & Lewin, S. P. (1994). Effectiveness of self-help and support groups for cancer patients. *Psychology and Health, 9*(6), 437-448.

Johnson, N. P., & Phelps, G. L. (1991). Effectiveness in self-help groups: Alcoholics Anonymous as a prototype. *Family and Community Health, 14*(1), 22-27.

Kolko, D. J., Loar, L. L., & Sturnick, D. (1990). Inpatient social skills training groups with conduct disordered and attention deficit disordered children. *Journal of Child Psychology and Psychiatry and Allied Discipline, 31*(5), 737-748.

Lieberman, M. (1990). A group therapist perspective on self-help groups. *International Journal of Group Psychotherapy, 40*(3), 251-278.

McKay, J. R., & Maisto, S. A. (1993). An overview and critique of advances in the treatment of alcohol use disorders. *Drugs and Society, 8*(1), 1-29.

Nash, K. B., & Kramer, K. D. (1993). Self-help for sickle cell disease in African-American communities. *Journal of Applied Behavioral Science, 29*(2), 202-215.

INDEX

ABOUT THE AUTHOR

Nina W. Brown, Ed.D., LPC, NCC, is a professor of counseling at Old Dominion University in Norfolk, Virginia. She received her doctorate from The College of William and Mary, and has taught at Old Dominion University since 1968.

Dr. Brown has published extensively in national journals on personality and other topics in the counseling discipline. Her specialty is group counseling, and she has three additional books published on group—*Teaching Group Dynamics: Process and Practice*; *Group Counseling for Elementary and Middle School Children*; and *Expressive Processes in Group Counseling*.

Dr. Brown resides in Virginia Beach, Virginia with her husband.